# NEW ESSAYS ON THE GRAPES OF WRATH

D0206344

★ The American Novel ★

GENERAL EDITOR

Emory Elliott
University of California, Riverside

Other books in the series:

Forthcoming:

# New Essays on
# The Grapes of Wrath

Edited by
David Wyatt

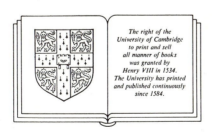

The right of the
University of Cambridge
to print and sell
all manner of books
was granted by
Henry VIII in 1534.
The University has printed
and published continuously
since 1584.

## CAMBRIDGE UNIVERSITY PRESS
*Cambridge*
*New York   Port Chester   Melbourne   Sydney*

Published by the Press Syndicate of the University of Cambridge
The Pitt Building, Trumpington Street, Cambridge CB2 1RP
40 West 20th Street, New York, NY 10011, USA
10 Stamford Road, Oakleigh, Melbourne 3166, Australia

First published 1990

Printed in the United States of America

*Library of Congress Cataloging-in-Publication Data*
New essays on The grapes of wrath / edited by David Wyatt.
p.   cm. – (The American novel)
Includes bibliographical references.
ISBN 0-521-36015-3. – ISBN 0-521-36909-6 (pbk.)
1. Steinbeck, John, 1902–1968. Grapes of wrath.   I. Wyatt,
David, 1948–   .  II. Series.
PS3537.T3234G857   1990
813'.52–dc20                                                          90–1338
                                                                          CIP

*British Library Cataloguing in Publication Data*
New essays on The grapes of wrath. – (The
American novel).
1. Fiction in English. American writers. Steinbeck, John,
1902–1968
I. Wyatt, David, *1948–*   II. Series
813.52

ISBN 0-521-36015-3 hardback
ISBN 0-521-36909-6 paperback

# Contents

v

# Contents

5

The Artful Propaganda of Ford's *The Grapes of Wrath*
LESLIE GOSSAGE

Notes on Contributors

Selected Bibliography

# Series Editor's Preface

In literary criticism the last twenty-five years have been particularly fruitful. Since the rise of the New Criticism in the 1950s, which focused attention of critics and readers upon the text itself – apart from history, biography, and society – there has emerged a wide variety of critical methods which have brought to literary works a rich diversity of perspectives: social, historical, political, psychological, economic, ideological, and philosophical. While attention to the text itself, as taught by the New Critics, remains at the core of contemporary interpretation, the widely shared assumption that works of art generate many different kinds of interpretation has opened up possibilities for new readings and new meanings.

Before this critical revolution, many American novels had come to be taken for granted by earlier generations of readers as having an established set of recognized interpretations. There was a sense among many students that the canon was established and that the larger thematic and interpretative issues had been decided. The task of the new reader was to examine the ways in which elements such as structure, style, and imagery contributed to each novel's acknowledged purpose. But recent criticism has brought these old assumptions into question and has thereby generated a wide variety of original, and often quite surprising, interpretations of the classics, as well as of rediscovered novels such as Kate Chopin's *The Awakening*, which has only recently entered the canon of works that scholars and critics study and that teachers assign their students.

The aim of The American Novel Series is to provide students of American literature and culture with introductory critical guides to

American novels now widely read and studied. Each volume is devoted to a single novel and begins with an introduction by the volume editor, a distinguished authority on the text. The introduction presents details of the novel's composition, publication history, and contemporary reception, as well as a survey of the major critical trends and readings from first publication to the present. This overview is followed by four or five original essays, specifically commissioned from senior scholars of established reputation and from outstanding younger critics. Each essay presents a distinct point of view, and together they constitute a forum of interpretative methods and of the best contemporary ideas on each text.

It is our hope that these volumes will convey the vitality of current critical work in American literature, generate new insights and excitement for students of the American novel, and inspire new respect for and new perspectives upon these major literary texts.

Emory Elliott
University of California, Riverside

# Note on the Text

The text used here is of the first edition of *The Grapes of Wrath*, published by Viking in 1939 in 619 pages. This text is most widely available in the Viking Critical Library edition (1972), edited by Peter Lisca. Lisca's edition also contains a chronology of Steinbeck's life, a map of the Joads' travels, a bibliography, and a collection of critical essays about the novel. All page references to *The Grapes of Wrath* in the essays printed in this volume have been adjusted to that edition and are included parenthetically in the text.

# 1

# Introduction

DAVID WYATT

I

IN America 1939 was a year of signs and portents, an ironist's *Annus Mirabilus*. A gleaming "World of Tomorrow" premiered in the borough of Queens, New York, four months before Germany invaded Poland. Hollywood roared through one of its all-time high production schedules with 483 movies, including *Wuthering Heights, Gone with the Wind,* and *The Wizard of Oz.* Meanwhile Broadway proved intent on records of its own: Clarence Day's *Life with Father* opened for a run of 3,244 performances. Ernest Hemingway completed his capstone novel about human solidarity, *For Whom the Bell Tolls,* while Granville Hicks resigned from the Communist Party. The world suddenly seemed within reach: Transatlantic air service started up, and television was first publicly broadcast. It was a time for connecting things: In Pasadena, ground was broken in the Arroyo Seco on the nation's first "freeway." It was also a time for splitting them apart: Albert Einstein wrote his letter to President Roosevelt, warning that "the element uranium may be turned into a new and important source of energy in the immediate future." The nation stood, as always, divided. When black contralto Marian Anderson tried to rent Constitution Hall, the DAR turned her down. Yet, whatever your politics, it was hard not to tap your foot at trumpeter Erskine Hawkins's new hit, "Tuxedo Junction." For people who were hungry, a food stamp program started in Rochester, New York; for those who were merely busy, the Bird's Eye label introduced the first line of precooked frozen food. The Works Progress Administration (WPA) received its last significant appropriation, and put out another score of its

1

unparalleled state guides. Pocket Books targeted a different market, bringing out 25-cent reprints of literary classics. The University of Chicago abandoned intercollegiate football, and hoped its peers would follow. An immigrating W. H. Auden sat in a bar on Fifty-Second Street and reviled the "low dishonest decade."

The biggest literary event of the year was the publication of John Steinbeck's *The Grapes of Wrath*. No American novel published in this century has aroused such a storm; one has to go back to *Uncle Tom's Cabin* to witness its equal. In November, 3 copies of the book were ritually burned in East St. Louis, Illinois. Viking shipped out 430,000 copies by the end of the year. "Critical reception" is for this novel too tame a term. People loved it or hated it, and scarcely knew why. Somehow it caught the bad faith and the good, the tensions of the time. Perhaps it spoke to the concern with how the parts of America fit into the whole.

Feeling ran highest in Oklahoma and California. Writing in 1944, Martin Shockley reported that *"The Grapes of Wrath* sold sensationally in Oklahoma bookstores. Most stores consider it their best seller, excepting *Gone with the Wind.* One bookstore in Tulsa reported about one thousand sales" (680).[1] Yet the state's newspapers drummed away on the theme of the book's veracity, accusing it of "complete and absurd untruthfulness" (683). Oklahoma Chambers of Commerce tried to stop the filming of John Ford's movie, and a California Hecklers Club was organized at the Mid Continent Petroleum Company in order properly to shift the blame. Congressman Lyle Boren called it a "dirty, filthy manuscript" (687). "Filthy" was a word that often came up, and from the perspective of fifty years it seems clear that the novel, in its earthiness and explicit sexuality, offended social decorum as much as or more than it did regional pride. As Walter Stein convincingly argues, "the chief criticism of *The Grapes of Wrath* was that it was obscene."[2]

Except in California, where the vital interests threatened by its vision were economic: There, the Associated Farmers orchestrated a statewide propaganda campaign. The tactic was not to rebut Steinbeck's charges but to supplant them with audacious fictions of benevolence. The titles tell all: Marshall Hartranft excogitated *Grapes of Gladness,* and the Kern County Chamber of Commerce launched plans for a film to rebut Ford's — *Plums of Plenty.* The most substantial response came from novelist Ruth Comfort Mitchell, whose 1940 *Of Human Kindness* contrasted the wanderlust of the Okies with the rooted discipline of an indigenous California farm family. Thus the forces arrayed against the novel followed the advice of the San Bernardino *Sun:* "The fallacy of this should hardly be dignified by a denial, it is so preposterous."[3]

The clamor reached even the White House. In 1940 President Roosevelt went on national radio to say that "I have read a book recently; it is called 'Grapes of Wrath.' There are 500,000 Americans that live in the covers of that book. I would like to see the Columbia Basin devoted to the care of the 500,000 people represented in 'Grapes of Wrath.' "[4] Eleanor was more succinct: "I never believed that *The Grapes of Wrath* was exaggerated" (B422).[5] Sweetest perhaps was the support of fellow Californian Upton Sinclair. "I remember how Elijah put his mantle on the shoulders of Elisha. John Steinbeck can have my old mantle if he has any use for it."[6] Writing in the *Herald Tribune,* Joseph Henry Jackson found the book "completely authentic."[7] Thus, even those who liked *The Grapes of Wrath* saw it as something that had to be defended as *true.* Stephen Railton's essay in this volume argues that the novel continues to be read as a radical critique, when it, instead, issues from a highly idiosyncratic and even visionary tradition of American political thought.

*The Grapes of Wrath* was first announced in *Publishers' Weekly* on December 31, 1938. Three advanced printings occurred before the novel actually appeared in March. The 619-page book cost $2.75. By April it was selling 2,500 copies a day; by May it reached the top of the best-seller list. Darryl Zanuck bought the screen rights for $75,000 that spring, and the movie opened nine months after the contract was signed. Overseas translations were quickly arranged in Danish, Dutch, French, Italian, Norwegian, Polish, Portuguese, Romanian, Swedish, and Russian, but the outbreak of war in Europe delayed the novel's wide distribution there. In 1940 the novel won both the National Book Award and the Pulitzer Prize. In his biography of Steinbeck, Brian St. Pierre notes of *The Grapes of Wrath* that "In 1982, the *New York Times* reported that it was the second-best-selling novel ever in paperback in America, with 14,600,000 copies printed."[8]

3

Professional literary critics took their cue from the tone of the public furor. As Peter Lisca argues: "One of the most striking aspects of critical writing about *The Grapes of Wrath* in its first fifteen years was its assertive nature. There is little analysis or detailed explication" (696). In his excellent Viking Critical Library edition, Lisca divides the pattern of response into this phase (1940–1955) and a second, more critical one, which culminated in the early 1970s. Lisca's edition appeared in 1972, and I follow his lead in arguing for a third phase of response to the novel which culminates with the publication of this volume. The event is by no means a conclusive one; in the academy, if not in the high schools, the status of *The Grapes of Wrath* remains uncertain. Despite its career as one of the two or three most widely sold and read classic American novels, it was not chosen by Cambridge University Press as one of the original ten to be featured in its American Novel series, and the intended release of this volume as part of a triad dealing with *A Separate Peace* and *The Catcher in the Rye* – a triad designed to *sell* – suggests that even those who believe in the book may still think of it as a *succès du scandal* rather than a *succès d'estime.*

These three phases of response, each of about fifteen years, can be roughly characterized as the Histrionic, the Formal, and the Contextual. In the first, the novel is subjected to a correspondence theory of truth that measures it against some putative social reality and the commentator against his or her political credentials. In the second, the novel provokes attention as a work of art that fulfills literary conventions and expectations. In the third, the novel is framed by its biographical and regional fields of force. The threefold pattern can be cast another way: Pretext (1940–1955); Text (1955–1973); and Context (1973–1989). Lisca's 1972 edition surveys the first two phases; this volume represents the concerns and achievements of the third.

### Pretext

Until the rise of New Criticism in the 1950s, the novel served commentators as a pretext for argument about social justice in the United States and even about the ultimate nature of humankind. Early reviewers focused on the extraliterary issue of anger. Malcolm Cowley claimed that the novel "belongs very high in the category of the great angry books like 'Uncle Tom's Cabin' that have roused a people to fight against intolerable wrongs."[9] *Atlantic* editor Edward Weeks saw in it "the summation of eighteen years of realism . . . a novel whose hunger, passion, and poetry are in direct answer to the angry stirring of our conscience these past seven years."[10] In his brilliant 1942 article called "California Pastoral," Carey McWilliams deployed the findings of the LaFollette Committee to show how they "verified the general picture of conditions in the state as set forth in *The Grapes of Wrath*" (658). McWilliams wrote in a tradition of debate instigated by articles like Frank J. Taylor's "California's Grapes of Wrath," which contained subheadings that read "No Joads Here" and claims that "no migrant family hungers in California unless it is too proud to accept relief" (644). The exceptions to this pattern – notably an essay by Frederic I. Carpenter – have proven the most durable as criticism. Carpenter widened the debate, to set the novel within three recurring strains in American intellectual history. "Here the mystical transcendentalism of Emerson reappears, and the earthy democracy of Whitman, and the pragmatic instrumentalism of William James and John Dewey" (709). Steinbeck's claim on us, Carpenter argues, has less to do with a crisis of the moment than with his revival of the authoritative voices of the past.

Carpenter's thoughtful study proved no match, however, for the firepower of Edmund Wilson. It was Wilson who set the terms of the initial critical debate, and he did so by casting Steinbeck as the crudest sort of naturalist. When he complained of Steinbeck's "tendency to present life in animal terms," or labeled his characters as "lemmings on their way to throw themselves into the sea,"[11] he protested against a vision of life that has frequently been assigned to Steinbeck, the vision of Frank Norris's Shelgrim, that stories deal "with forces . . . not with men." The debate about Steinbeck's literary naturalism continues, most notably in Donald Pizer's 1982 *Twentieth-Century American Literary Naturalism*, which redefines the mode into one so capacious that few readers would feel troubled by its limitations. Yet the expansion was one Steinbeck insisted on from the start, and in a piece of self-criticism that shows how writers may sometimes prove their best readers.

In 1939 Steinbeck sent friend and reviewer Joseph Henry Jackson some suggestions for an interview. Both the tone and the imagery in these proposed questions and answers suggest that Steinbeck had concerned himself as much with a mythic vision of America as with actual conditions. "I have set down what a large section of our people are doing and wanting, and symbolically what all people of all time are doing and wanting" (859). His characters are not lemmings, but dreamers, drawn by the power of what he calls "westering." He has written a novel about *desire,* and "this migration is the outward sign of the want" (859). Borrowing his model from the French mythographer Boileau, Steinbeck imagines time as a falling off from the Age of "Kings, Gods, and Heroes" (861) to the present Age of the Poor. The model imposes a pattern on time, one that implies the possibility of an upward swing, of redemption. It is a model meant to ease the heart, and so reveals Steinbeck as more beholden to Northrop Frye's theory of literary modes than to journalistic fact. The next phase of criticism would reveal him as possessed by a tradition that protected him from the reductions implicit in any consciously held social doctrine.

*Text*

Criticism in the 1950s and 1960s shifted attention to the patterns *The Grapes of Wrath* contained within itself, to its autonomy and shape as a text. During this period the book received its most intense reading as a piece of writing. Major full-length studies of Steinbeck were published by Lisca, Warren French, and Howard Levant. The Viking Critical Library edition appeared in 1972 and Walter Stein published his authoritative *California and the Dust Bowl Migration* in 1973.

Lisca dates this phase from French's "Another Look at *The Grapes of Wrath,*" the 1955 response to Bernard Bowron's "Wagons West" thesis. Bowron had argued that the book appeals because it borrows its shape from the myth of the Overland Trail. French set Steinbeck's novel within a more venerable tradition of journeying, one established in the Bible and *The Odyssey.* The rising tide of

6

imagery studies soon took up French's suggestion; parallels between the novel and the Bible had often been remarked, and, as Lisca puts it, "an exploration of this symbolism" (700) was now to lead the way. The most compelling of these efforts was J. P. Hunter's 1963 essay, "Steinbeck's Wine of Affirmation in *The Grapes of Wrath.*" Hunter convincingly demonstrates that in the novel's ending "the Bible's three major symbols of a purified order are suggested: the Old Testament deluge, the New Testament stable, and the continuing ritual of communion" (812–13). Hunter thus not only establishes Steinbeck's art of allusion but also makes a case for the coherence of the novel's most controversial formal feature, its sudden ending in the marooned barn.

During this period Peter Lisca and Warren French emerged as the two leading Steinbeck critics, and they have proven the most sympathetic keepers of the flame. Lisca's 1958 *The Wide World of John Steinbeck* became the standard critical study, while French's 1961 *John Steinbeck* transcended the typically flat-footed Twayne series format with a moving thesis about the Joads' "education of the heart." Lisca's 1957 *PMLA* article on "*The Grapes of Wrath* as Fiction" marked his key contribution to the appreciation of the novel as a form. "Steinbeck's great achievement in *The Grapes of Wrath* is that while minimizing what seem to be the most essential elements of fiction – plot and character – he was able to create a well-made and emotionally compelling novel out of materials which in most other hands have resulted in sentimental propaganda" (757). French went on to contribute two *Companions* to Steinbeck studies – *The Grapes of Wrath* as a novel, and as a movie – that remain concise and useful anthologies.

Stein's 1973 book on California and the Dust Bowl argued for the power of advertising and romantic ideology as motive forces in the migration and provided the best ten pages available on the immediate reaction to Steinbeck's novel. But the major event of the year was the publication of Howard Levant's *The Novels of John Steinbeck: A Critical Study.* French's Introduction to the book calls it a "turning point in Steinbeck studies."[12] Levant's was a formalist approach that saw in Steinbeck's career "a constant but changing search for harmony between structure and materials."[13] The harmony is rarely sustained, or achieved. Levant's disappointment with *The Grapes of Wrath* is particularly acute:

> The first three quarters of the novel are masterful. Characters are presented through action; the central theme of transformation from self to group develops persuasively in a solid, realized documentary context. The final quarter of the novel presents a difference in every respect. Characters are fitted or forced into allegorical roles, heightened beyond the limits of credibility, to the point that they thin out or become frankly unbelievable. Scenes are developed almost solely as links in an allegorical pattern. Texture is reduced to documentation, and allegorical signs replace symbolism.[14]

If Steinbeck's novel proves here a technical failure, it has at least been taken as a venture with technique. And if Levant's view links him with a tradition of strong critics who wring their hands before the mystery of Steinbeck's power – witness R. W. B. Lewis's lament about a career that "has the shape of a suggestive, a representative, and a completely honorable failure"[15] – it is also the most thoroughly argued negative case, one that stands as a challenge to all future criticism.

*Context*

In 1975 Elaine Steinbeck and Robert Wallsten published *Steinbeck: A Life in Letters,* a nearly 900-page edition of the novelist's correspondence, with bridging notes. Suddenly the life seemed within view; the first biography was not to appear until 1979. The collection remains invaluable, but it is by no means complete, and some of the letters have been edited with no indication as to the extent or even the fact of the ellision. The edition is largely a protective enterprise. Thomas Kiernan's *The Intricate Music: A Biography of John Steinbeck* followed four years later. It is a convenient short chronicle, somewhat hastily written. The most significant book still to appear on Steinbeck – the best book yet to appear – was Jackson Benson's 1984 biography, *The True Adventures of John Steinbeck, Writer.*

By "Writer" Benson does not mean to call up *écriture,* the dispersal of the self through words. The story he tells is of writing as a profession and a moral and emotional effort. Steinbeck's struggle with words is the center of his story. The composition of *The Grapes of Wrath* permanently took something from Steinbeck, just as it gave something to the world. As the following pages will show, all of those who would tell that story must rely on Benson.

Benson's Steinbeck is a thinker as well as a writer, and so the biography is also a history of his ideas. Benson depicts Steinbeck as a biological thinker "whose affection for the alternative to an anthropocentric view of life is unique" (B244). His Steinbeck is a man of coherent philosophy who seeks to express it as a theme in his fiction. The philosophy – be it "non-teleological thinking" or the "phalanx" theory – maintains that a human can see but not change the world: One is a cell in a larger body. Benson's is a masterful account, but, as in any search for a coherent life story, it cannot give full play to the ways in which images, tones, and situations in the novels and stories qualify or contradict Steinbeck's announced philosophies.

These biographies and editions provided critics the chance to align the "long structure" of his work, as Steinbeck called it, with his personal history.[16] But the mythology of his region worked its influence on him as well, and six books published since 1973 argue for the importance of Steinbeck's California origins. Kevin Starr published the first volume in his prize-winning *Americans and the California Dream* series in 1973. *Inventing the Dream* followed in 1985. Currently at work on the third volume in the series, on California's Depression years, Starr has summoned the deep background against which to understand Steinbeck's profoundly regional achievement.

William Everson's *Archetype West: The Pacific Coast as a Literary Region* (1976) gave Steinbeck a central place in its argument that California writers resolve their stories through acts of apotheosized violence. "Man is the intelligence of his soil," as Wallace Stevens has remarked. Brian St. Pierre pursued the corollary thesis, one also put forth by Stevens: "The soil is man's intelligence." His *John Steinbeck: The California Years* (1983) argues the standard conclusion about Steinbeck's departure for the East after finishing *The Grapes of Wrath*: "He had drawn his strength as an artist from his native soil and, like Antaeus of Greek myth, he had lost it when he left it."[17] The felt tension in Steinbeck's consciousness between

East and West is the subject of Louis Owens's *John Steinbeck's Re-Vision of America* (1985). Behind Steinbeck's work "lies a profound fascination with and acute sensitivity to California's place in the American consciousness."[18] For Owens, the Joads' fate proves that the West, and California in particular, became for Steinbeck destinations of failed promise. My own book, *The Fall into Eden: Landscape and Imagination in California* (1986), attempts to place Steinbeck within a regional tradition of discovering a self by describing a landscape. The gathering force of this body of criticism has been to establish, against Wilson's hasty 1941 judgments, that "the writer on the Coast" has found a way to capture the adventure of California, "to struggle with new phases of experience, and to give them beauty and sense."[19]

The third phase of Steinbeck criticism has corresponded to the rise of theory in the academy and to the proliferation of engaged approaches to literature: feminism, deconstruction, the new historicism. Steinbeck's work is just beginning to be re-evaluated in light of these new approaches. Its surface simplicity and principled avoidance of irony make it difficult to appropriate to any critical program. One way forward has been through a traditional critical strategy, the comparison. In "Imagining Existence: Form and History in Steinbeck and Agee," Linda Ray Pratt contrasts *The Grapes of Wrath* as a documentary to *Let Us Now Praise Famous Men.* Steinbeck's content is "cultural myth"; Agee's, "the divinity of humanity." Pratt's clear preference for Agee leaves her dismissing Steinbeck's novel as "an easy entertainment, requiring little from us in the reading and letting us off at the end with a symbolic gesture that is an escape from reality."[20] In her *In Visible Light: Photography and the American Writer, 1840–1940,* Carol Shloss explores the morality of looking into and making images out of the lives of the oppressed. Shloss compares Steinbeck unfavorably to Dorothea Lange, and concludes that "Though Steinbeck had sought to recodify a relation of force, using fiction as the displaced voice of the dispossessed, he ended by reduplicating the power structure he thought he was criticizing."[21] In the following pages William Howarth explores the origins of Steinbeck's "documentary" style and places him within a context of achievement in which a more positive judgment becomes possible.

10

Steinbeck's prolonged relationship with Hollywood has provoked many accounts of his work and the movies, most notably Joseph Millichap's *Steinbeck and Film* (1983). Millichap sees the relationship as contributing to Steinbeck's post-*Grapes* decline: "one cause of Steinbeck's literary achievement, as well as his decline, is his relationship to film."[22] Leslie Gossage's essay in this volume takes a less positivistic view. She argues for John Ford's film as a text with a complexity of its own, with a visual rhetoric that involves its American audience in a conflict between distance and identification.

The vision of women in Steinbeck's work has usually received negative notice: They are so often the objects of male fantasy, desire, or anxiety. In "From Patriarchy to Matriarchy: Ma Joad's Role in *The Grapes of Wrath*," Warren Motley detects a dependence on "the collective security of matriarchal society rather than on patriarchal self-reliance."[23] Nellie McKay's essay, published here, questions whether Steinbeck's novel can be read as a fantasy of cooperation rather than power. Hers is an important contribution to the growing sense that even America's most stubbornly "male" texts can be read as speaking to audiences their rhetoric and politics might seem to exclude.


## II

The years in which Steinbeck researched and wrote *The Grapes of Wrath* culminated in the greatest personal upheaval in his life. The themes of the period are fame, divorce, and departure: By 1941 he had lost his privacy, his wife, and his home state. Many readers have noted a falling off in the quality of Steinbeck's work after the publication of his greatest novel, and these crises have been summoned to explain it. Jackson Benson explores them all in his capacious and sympathetic biography. But the question of Steinbeck's "decline" — that midlife failure of vision of which we accuse so many American writers — he links directly with the nature of Steinbeck's success. The project became a self-consuming one: "Critics and literary historians have speculated about what happened to change Steinbeck after *The Grapes of Wrath*. One answer is that what happened was the writing of the novel itself" (B392).

The "widening of concern" experienced by the Joad family also overtook Steinbeck in the 1930s. During the early years of the decade he devoted himself to writing and took scant interest in politics. The famous debates with Ed Ricketts and friends on Cannery Row stuck mainly to "speculative metaphysics" (B196). As the decade waned, however, Steinbeck's journalistic assignments drew him ever deeper into the fate of his culture, and especially toward those who had been discarded by it. Steinbeck's adolescent loathing of respectability transformed itself during these years into an active compassion for the dispossessed. And the personal shocks of the 1930s also left him with a cheerfully curtailed sense of his own superior virtue, as an unpublished letter written in 1941 suggests:

> I must have got from my father (a man who never lived fully until it came his time to die) a feeling that I should so live and think and act that I could admire myself, that I could feel that I was just and good and decent. I tried that for a long time. There's no better way of cutting oneself off. Now I don't admire myself at all and I know I have been unjust and not good and decent and far from being a bad thing it makes me feel very much related to people and things. If I can grow through these things to actually like myself that will be good.[24]

The major inclusive motion of *The Grapes of Wrath* thus re-enacts Steinbeck's own "education of the heart."

In the spring of 1935 Steinbeck first mentioned plans for a "big book" (B316). Money coming in from royalties and the film sale of *Tortilla Flat*, along with a portion of his father's estate, would soon make possible a long-range plan. His involvement with California labor problems had begun a year earlier, when he had met with two fugitive strike organizers and agreed to pay them for their stories. The result was *In Dubious Battle*. After the publication of the novel, members of the John Reed Club and the Young Communist League began dropping by the house. He formed a friendship with a Carmel neighbor, muckraking journalist Lincoln Steffens. His relation to the politics of his story remained, however, a distant one.

> I have used a small strike in an orchard valley as the symbol of man's eternal, bitter warfare with himself. I'm not interested in

strike as a means of raising men's wages, and I'm not interested in ranting about justice and oppression, mere outcroppings which indicate the condition (L98).

He insisted upon maintaining his modest ego-ideal, a writer in search of a story. The turning point came in May, 1936, when George West of the *San Francisco News* paid Steinbeck a visit. As the paper's chief editorial writer, West was looking to commission a series of articles on California's migrant workers. Steinbeck agreed, fixed up an old bakery truck, and, accompanied by an ex-preacher and now regional director in the migrant camp program, took off. They drove down the Central Valley and stopped at Hoovervilles and government demonstration camps along the way. Steinbeck now had what his sensibility demanded: the shock of first-hand observation. The accuracy of Steinbeck's account of conditions has been debated for fifty years. Perhaps the last word in the matter should be left to Carey McWilliams, who published *Factories in the Fields* in the same year as Steinbeck's novel: "Mr. Steinbeck, in *The Grapes of Wrath*, was not relying on his imagination" (679).

At a place called Weedpatch, near the bottom of the valley, Steinbeck met a man named Tom Collins. The first camp manager in California, Collins became the model for the sympathetic Jim Rawley, as well as the object of the novel's dedication. Chapter 22 represents his achievements quite accurately. Collins became more than an inspiration and traveling companion for Steinbeck; he shared with him his long reports to the Resettlement Administration, and they provided the novelist with a fund of migrant behavior and lore.

Steinbeck's seven articles for the *News* appeared in the fall of 1936 and were gathered together two years later in the pamphlet *Their Blood Is Strong*. He also started a version of the big book entitled "L'Affaire Lettuceberg," an angry attack on economic conditions in his own Salinas Valley. A trip to Europe intervened before he could return to his California materials, as did a stop in New York where he was forced to play the role of "a fifth-rate celebrity" (B356) in the brouhaha over the best-selling *Of Mice and Men*. On the return from the East John and Carol drove home along Route 66.

13

In October, 1937, Steinbeck took another trip to the Central Valley and met with Collins at his new camp at Gridley. The two men agreed to go out and work in the fields. The evidence is sketchy, but they may have traveled as far south as the Imperial Valley. Back at Los Gatos his arrival was celebrated as "a return from Oklahoma" – a rehearsal for the odyssey of the Joads – and he let the legend stand. Perhaps the most important of Steinbeck's missions occurred in the following February, when he went to Visalia to see Collins again. The area had been ravaged by terrible floods, and together they spent two sleepless days dragging stranded people to higher ground. The experience did a lot to unsettle a man skeptical about the efficacy of "one person's effort" (B371).

Steinbeck now went home and began to write. (In 1989 Viking published the journals Steinbeck kept while writing the novel. *Working Days,* edited by Robert DeMott, provides the scholar with ready access to Steinbeck's remarkably self-conscious habits of composition.) He told his agent that "I'm trying to write history while it is happening and I don't want to be wrong" (B375). The draft of 60,000 words was finished by early May, and it was still called "Lettuceberg." But it was "pretty badly done," and liable, Steinbeck worried, to "cause hatred through partial understanding" (B376). Carol called it "a series of cartoons caricaturing Salinas fat cats" (B348). Steinbeck knew that he had to fuse his anger with his compassion, and knew that he had not done it. So he burned the manuscript.

That summer he started again and tried to adopt a slow and steady pace, like a turtle. The second half of 1938 was when *The Grapes of Wrath* got written. The pace quickened, and soon he was racing like a hare, sometimes writing all night. By August there came the first signs of a nervous collapse, as he admitted in his journal: "8/1 My nerves are very bad, awful in fact. . . . Don't know who will publish my book" (B379). Carol had strep throat, his publisher was going bankrupt, he was mired in the purchase of a new ranch. On September 3, Carol came up with a title, and it stuck: "9/3 Carol got the title last night *The Grapes of Wrath.* I think that is a wonderful title. . . . The book has being at last" (B379–80). It was the last significant product of his marriage, and in the dedication he gave Carol ample credit: "To CAROL who willed this book."

The years of Steinbeck's first marriage were his growing years, especially as a writer. Benson calls them the years of Poverty and Success. John had met Carol Henning in the summer of 1928 while working at a fish hatchery in the Sierra Nevada. They were married in 1930. Carol supported him faithfully in his career, from laboring as his typist to acting as his most trusted critic. They lived a mildly bohemian life until the income of the late 1930s catapulted them into the middle class. With money and fame came the tensions of ownership, and as their marriage resolved into a dispute about how and where to live, husband and wife were driven apart.

In his brief biography, Thomas Kiernan ventures one interpretation of Steinbeck's broken first marriage. Husband and wife came to grief over Carol's attachment to the ranch near Los Gatos:

> Where before she had been content to live under the plainest of conditions and in the simplest of surroundings, now she seemed to aspire more and more to all those middle-class values that he had long despised. . . . Upon settling in at the remote ranch, it was as if she had attained the pinnacle of her life's ambition. She was content to live the secure, quiet existence afforded by the ranch and to gather about her all the things that would provide them with comfortable self-sufficiency. In transforming herself in this way, she subtly demanded the same form of contentment and satisfaction from John.[25]

The Steinbecks had first moved to Los Gatos in 1936, to a modest and isolated house in the forested hills. They bought the nearby fifty-acre Biddle Ranch two years later. While the big new house with the pool for Carol went up, the Steinbecks were reduced to living in a decayed farmhouse on the new property – in a kind of boxcar of their own. During the final months of his work on *The Grapes of Wrath*, Steinbeck was literally without a home, and by the completion of the manuscript he was "in a state of total collapse" (B388).

John's publisher had recently moved to Viking, and in January the press sent out Elizabeth Otis, John's trusted agent, to help him clean up the book's language. For two days they fought and revised while John nursed an infected leg. The expurgated text had to be dictated to Western Union over the phone. A second flap with Viking over the closing scene provoked from Steinbeck one of his most eloquent moments of self-defense. The ending had struck the group-mind in New York "as being too abrupt" (B390). Steinbeck replied to Pascal Covici:

> I have your letter today. And I am sorry but I cannot change the ending. It is casual – there is no fruity climax, it is not more important than any other part of the book – if there is a symbol, it is a survival symbol not a love symbol, it must be an accident, it must be a stranger, and it must be quick. (B390)

What Steinbeck did not know was that a major phase in his own life – certainly the most creative phase – was also ending, although it would not be quick.

John's new money began to separate him from his old friends. Drinking and fights with Carol increased. Life became a round of celebrities – Charlie Chaplin often dropped by – and retreat from them. John was nervous over local reaction to his book. Years later he told a friend that the undersheriff of Santa Clara County had warned him not to go into a hotel room alone. "The boys got a rape case set up for you. You get alone in a hotel and a dame will come in, tear off her clothes, scratch her face and scream and you try to talk yourself out of that one. They won't touch your book but there's easier ways" (L187). Benson argues that "The whole atmosphere of the house appeared to change, decline, even become corrupt, during the months that followed the publication of *Grapes* and on through the succeeding year. It was as if John's worst fears about fame and money were coming true" (B416). John met Gwyndolyn Conger in June 1939, and arranged his first separation from Carol in August. During the next two years he wavered between the wife and the chorus girl, finally choosing not only for Gwyn but for a life with her in New York. There he could escape the dreaded publicity and the still intense hostility his work had aroused, as well as leaving Carol some room to move. He was sick of controversy and had already turned to work on explicit biological rather than political themes. When he left for New York in the fall of 1941 his life in the West was done; although he would return and even live there briefly again, he had stopped believing that California was his unique and necessary home.

## III

*The Grapes of Wrath* occupies a signal position in Steinbeck's career. It is the last book of his great decade. Like Hemingway (Steinbeck was three years younger), Steinbeck seemed to lose stride once the Second World War began. By 1939 he had seven books behind him, all strong performances except for his first, the historical swashbuckler *Cup of Gold* (1929). After the story of the Joads he would publish ten more books, and would stray into projects like the search for Malory's Arthur. None of these books would match the achievements of the 1930s. Honors would come – the Nobel Prize in 1962 – but not, with them, the sure sense that they were any longer deserved. It is as if by 1940 Steinbeck had worked something through, and was done with it.

Steinbeck's best work naturalizes in his home state the central Western legend of loss. During the 1930s he wrote a series of books that deal, in sequence, with the acts of settlement, corruption, fall, and eviction. *The Grapes of Wrath* is the last of these, and California is the garden lost. Steinbeck treats his birthplace as a natural and imaginative fact. Although its specific locales and landscapes shape the course of a story's action, its location on a map of the mind converts it into a kind of national or even global destiny, the end point of humanity's incessant "westering." Steinbeck's contribution to the literature of his nation and his region is to discover ways in which the unique features and history of a place can be discreetly raised up toward the status of myth.

Steinbeck's best books try and usually fail to establish a garden that can be shared by the sexes; the lesser works are linked by their will to literalize a paradise of men. Wanderlust is the option by which his strong characters are repeatedly tempted; the choice is between home and the road. His lesser characters so easily resolve this tension – in favor of home – that we may doubt the offered resolution. What their stories give us, in fact, are pseudo-homes, places in the sun empty of the women who could give them eros,

17

and tension, and continuity. The fantasy gets fully realized in "Breakfast," the last story completed in *The Long Valley,* the book Steinbeck published while finishing *The Grapes of Wrath.*

"Breakfast" is a story of uncanny hospitality, of a wanderer happening on a moment of domestic bliss in the middle of nowhere:

> It was very early in the morning. The eastern mountains were black-blue, but behind them the light stood up faintly colored at the mountain rims with a washed red, growing colder, greyer and darker as it went up and overhead until, at a place near the west, it merged with pure night.
>
> And it was cold, not painfully so, but cold enough so that I rubbed my hands and shoved them deep into my pockets, and I hunched my shoulders up and scuffled my feet on the ground. Down in the valley where I was, the earth was that lavender grey of dawn. I walked along a country road and ahead of me I saw a tent that was only a little lighter grey than the ground. Beside the tent there was a flash of orange fire seeping out of the cracks of an old rusty iron stove. Grey smoke spurted up out of the stubby stovepipe, spurted up a long way before it spread out and dissipated.
>
> I saw a young woman beside the stove, really a girl. (LV85-6)[26]

She holds a baby in the crook of her arm. The wanderer approaches:

> I was close now and I could smell frying bacon and baking bread, the warmest, pleasantest odors I know. From the east the light grew swiftly. I came near to the stove and stretched my hands out to it and shivered all over when the warmth struck me. (LV86)

He is welcomed like an old friend, yet no one knows or speaks any names:

> "Had your breakfast?"
> "No."
> "Well, sit down with us, then." (LV87)

He arrives, eats, and leaves. "And I walked away down the country road" (LV88).

It is the quality of his memory that puzzles the speaker here. "I don't know why, I can see it in the smallest detail. I find myself recalling it again and again, each time bringing more detail out of sunken memory, remembering brings the curious warm pleasure"

18

(LV85). What he comes upon when he remembers is a universal human bequest liberated from location and history, a primal warmth innocent of identity and relationship. To establish this warmth in a place where people call each other by name – in a home – is the difficult task of *The Grapes of Wrath*. The Joads begin as family-bound provincials. They go on to reform a jealously guarded intimacy into one where no one is a stranger. Warren French calls this process the "education of the heart"; J. P. Hunter has shown how the "widening of concern" culminates in Rose of Sharon's offer of her breast. The movement is outward toward larger and more inclusive structures, "from 'I' to 'we' " (206).

*The Grapes of Wrath* also marks the end of Steinbeck's conception of home as a place. The opening up of the family corresponds to a movement west in which the Joads discover the human power of indwelling. This is the power Tom invokes in his farewell speech, one he makes after finding that California will not provide his family a localized home. This promised land resists all attempts at entry, and so inspires, through its economic and geographical inaccessibility, a sublimation of the will to settle into citizenship in an immaterial domain of belonging.

Locating the first third of the action on the road is the book's major imaginative act. Steinbeck begins his book outside that "valley of the world" (L73) – California – that he had so carefully cultivated during the 1930s as the site for his best work. We start east of Eden, and the book becomes a struggle to reenter a paradise from which we have become separated by space, if not divorced by the very nature of time. We begin with loss and move toward the possibility of gain. This is Steinbeck's first wholly postlapsarian book, one that focuses on the consequences of rather than the imminence of fall. Humanity is now stationed in the middle rather than at the beginning of history, and wandering is no longer a male but a human prerogative.

Peter Lisca argues that in *The Grapes of Wrath* Steinbeck moralizes the necessity of motion. He reads the ongoing turtle as an embodiment of "the indomitable life force" that "drives the Joads" (733). Life here does seem equipped and therefore perhaps intended for motion rather than fixity. It is "armed with an appliance of dispersal" and possessed of the "anlage of movement" (20). The travel-readiness of the vegetable and animal worlds is met, however, by a reluctance to move in the human one – "They're just goddamn sick of goin' " (15) – and the motion into which the Joads are propelled may be less a behavior affirmed than a condition to which they must adapt. When Steinbeck argues in Chapter 14 that the California migration is a "result," not a "cause" (204), he defines that movement as a function of a state of dispossession, though one more primal than eviction from an Oklahoma farm.

For what *The Grapes of Wrath* imagines is a world without origins or ends, one in which archaeological thinking is no more appropriate than teleological thinking. Its characters believe that they have only temporarily given in to the road: "Folks out lonely on the road, folks with no lan', no home to go to. They got to have some kind of home" (76). But the novel never delivers more than a momentary stay against the confusion of moving on. A human is the thing always on the way, and "way" becomes the word that here takes in the emerging sense of the finality of death and the uncertainty of life.

Casy begins as a man who wants to lead the people somewhere. Tom wonders why: "What the hell you want to lead 'em some place for? Jus' lead 'em" (29). Steinbeck undercuts Tom's non-teleological thinking by having the narrative suddenly produce a goal-bound dog: "A thick-furred yellow shepherd dog came trotting down the road, head low, tongue lolling and dripping. . . . Joad whistled at it, but it only dropped its head an inch and trotted fast toward some definite destination. 'Goin' someplace,' Joad explained, a little piqued. 'Goin' for home maybe' " (29). The joke on Tom reminds us of the tenacity of those nostalgias the novel cannot requite. As the journey west unfolds, Casy reluctantly discards the hope for an end. "Seems to me we don't never come to nothin'. Always on the way" (173). The experience of the way comes to dominate the imaginations of the major characters – Tom, Casy, and Ma. While they elaborate an understanding of the "way" out of their unique historical moment, this emerging vision universalizes itself into something akin to "the human condition." Like that other great book about westering toward California,

George Stewart's *Ordeal by Hunger* (1936), *The Grapes of Wrath* becomes a study of human thrownness in which the act of moving through a landscape images an infinite and ever-receding supply. Steinbeck seems to have set himself the task of recovering the story of California's repulsion of the Donners in his own place and time. In both stories the human "way" has only one sure end, and our view of it remains obscured:

> This here ol' man jus' lived a life and jus' died out of it. I don' know whether he was good or bad, but that don't matter much. He was alive, an' that's what matters. An' now he's dead, an' that don't matter. . . . He's awright. He got a job to do, but it's all laid out for 'im an' there's on'y one way to do it. But us, we got a job to do, an' they's a thousan' ways, an' we don' know which one to take. (196–7)

Despite the certainty of death, the uncertainty of how to approach it converts life into an end-less or open-ended way. *The Grapes of Wrath* is not just a book about the difficult "way" to California; its subtle rhetoric generalizes the project into the problem of learning to live in existential time.

The very book in which Steinbeck fully establishes the claims and appeal of "home" is thus also the one in which he renders such places illusory or untenable. This is most strikingly demonstrated in his return to the fantasy of "Breakfast." Steinbeck incorporates the story into the middle of Chapter 22. Tom Joad has now become its protagonist. He wanders in and out of the story in a way that registers a dramatic shift in Steinbeck's attitude toward human destinations.

The core of the fantasy remains unchanged; we come upon the tent in the dawn, the promise of warmth, the nursing woman and her two men, the easy offer of a meal. But Tom here comes out of somewhere – the moving and dwindling solidarity that the Joad family has become. When asked if he has eaten, the first thing Tom thinks of is the others: "Well, no, I ain't. But my folks is over there" (396). And he comes with the intention to work. In "Breakfast" the wanderer's answer to the question "Picking cotton?" had been a simple "No" (LV87). Tom's answer to the same question is "Aim to" (397). When the men offer to "get" him "on," the wanderer says, "No. I got to go along" (LV88). Tom says, "Well, that's mighty nice of you" (398). The sudden generosity of the world survives here, then, and fulfills itself in a purpose more abiding than the lovely pleasures of the moment. There is no walking "away down the country road." Instead, Tom returns to his tent, alerts Ruthie, and walks out to earn his bread with the sweat of his brow.

The pathos of this episode is that it refuses to become, for the Joads, more than a short story. The warmth and hope it offers are too temporary to cast anything more than an ironic light on the surrounding text. We happen on an ecstasy no longer attractive or credible to Steinbeck; now he wants to earn such grace. But earning a home is precisely what this world will not allow, and our appetite is aroused only to have our hunger unappeased.

"Breakfast" ends with an epiphany of light, and this too anticipates a crucial structure of imagery in the later novel:

> The two men faced the east and their faces were lighted by the dawn, and I looked up for a moment and saw the image of the mountain and the light coming over it reflected in the older man's eyes. (LV88)

A man looking at men looking at the light: Of what is this a figure except for the writer himself? There is a kind of phototropism in Steinbeck; his characters seem congenitally drawn toward the light. Light is the thing outside, a figure for our exposure in a world under the sun. Steinbeck's light movingly renders the pathos of our necessary submission to the rhythm of a day. Getting up and going to sleep engage us in a mortal drama, what in *East of Eden* he calls "the death and birth of the day."[27] Sunrise and sunset receive his constant attention. *The Grapes of Wrath* begins with a desperate struggle to keep the sun in the sky: "The dawn came, but no day. In the grey sky a red sun appeared, a dim red circle that gave a little light" (5). As Tom approaches home a "lonely dawn" (93) creeps up, and Pa can barely see him against the rising light. Morning is the "good time" (93) in Steinbeck, the moment of promise, but the day itself, with the sun that strikes at noon, or disappears at night like "a bloody rag" (65), calls forth all our reservoirs of patience and endurance. As light strikes, warms, blinds, and disappears, it seems a force wholly beyond us, a figure for all the power we do not have.

Yet when the crisis of the novel comes, it is a crisis of light, man-made light. Someone stands up amid the "lanterns and torches." "Casy stared blindly at the light" (527). In this climactic scene, a good man is brought down in a confusion of human lights, a scene set up 400 pages earlier by the "bar of cold white light" (80) playing over an abandoned farm. Casy and Tom and Muley had then been "scairt to get in the light" (80); now, the hero steps willingly into it. "He was jus' standin' there with the lights on' 'im" (535). It is Casy's political illumination that compels him into the "flashlight beams" (527); the novel in fact traces a steady growth in the human power to internalize and manipulate the light. Thus, when Ma visits Tom a last time in his "lightless" cave, they are not cut off by any literal dark. "I wanta touch ya again, Tom. It's like I'm blin', it's so dark. I wanta remember, even if it's only my fingers that remember" (569). She uses her hands to see his face; there is finally no need for a further light. The next morning she gets up in "the lightless car" (580), shivers, rubs her hands.

> She crept back and fumbled for the matches, beside the lantern. The shade screeched up. She lighted the wick, watched it burn blue for a moment and then put up its yellow, delicately curved ring of light. She carried the lantern to the stove and set it down while she broke the brittle dry willow twigs into the fire box. In a moment the fire was roaring up the chimney.

This is the heart of Steinbeck's vision, and has become, by *The Grapes of Wrath*, not only a figure for pleasure but for courage: a woman cooking breakfast. When Ma gets up and moves to the lantern and the stove, she measures how far she has and has not traveled, no farther perhaps than from the bedroom to the kitchen in that daily, anonymous ritual in which we get out of bed, rub our eyes, light up the world.

Instead of a local habitation with a name, then, *The Grapes of Wrath* offers a reformation of the lonely ecstasies in which his earlier characters stood imprisoned. Isolating self-consciousness is raised up, as Tom broods on a shared homelessness and a potential human solidarity, into an invulnerable realm of concern. We no longer try to occupy a spot, but survive, through love and imagina-

tion, in an "everywhere." Tom takes leave of his mother, but it is
really impossible to say good-bye:

> I'll be all aroun' in the dark. I'll be ever'where – wherever you look.
> Wherever they's a fight so hungry people can eat, I'll be there.
> Wherever they's a cop beatin' up a guy, I'll be there. If Casy
> knowed, why, I'll be in the way guys yell when they're mad an' –
> I'll be in the way kids laugh when they're hungry an' they know
> supper's ready. An' when our folks eat the stuff they raise an' live in
> the houses they build – why, I'll be there. (572)

This speech marks the culmination of Steinbeck's major phase. He
has learned the value of home while losing belief in the possibility
of it. The strong books of the thirties move toward Tom's qualified
affirmation, one in which Steinbeck naturalizes the great myth of
the West in *his* West. Tom appeals to the time-honored consolation
for the loss of an earthly garden. As a departing Adam stands at the
gates of Eden, Michael comforts him with the promise that if he
adds love to faith, he will come to "possess / A paradise within
thee, happier far." The beauty of the episode lies in the dreaming
Eve's simultaneous incorporation of the promise, an act that enables her to voice, as she wakes to depart with her husband, the
poem's radical insight about the relation of person to place. In a
world where the wind is finally left to farm the dust, there is still
left us the unlocalized garden of human love: "all places thou."
Eve then takes Adam by the hand, and they begin walking. If they
look back, they look back to see a flaming brand over paradise, the
way an Oklahoma family would one day look back at a receding
home to see "the windows reddening under the first color of the
sun" (156). Walking becomes their destination and their destiny,
and the world in which they seek "Thir place of rest" resolves
itself, not into a vale of privileged sites, but, in the last word of
Milton's poem and the key word in Steinbeck's book, into a "way."

## NOTES

1. The quote is from Peter Lisca's Viking Critical Library edition of *The
   Grapes of Wrath* (1972), p. 680. Subsequent references to pages in this
   volume will be included as parenthetical numbers in the text.

24

2. Walter J. Stein, *California and the Dust Bowl Migration* (Westport, CT: Greenwood Press, 1973), p. 206.

3. Warren French, *A Companion to the Grapes of Wrath* (New York: Viking, 1963), p. 117.

4. Stein, p. 209.

5. Jackson J. Benson, *The True Adventures of John Steinbeck, Writer* (New York: Viking, 1984), p. 422. Subsequent references to pages in this volume will be abbreviated as "B" and included as parenthetical numbers in the text.

6. Stein, p. 203.

7. French, p. 114.

8. Brian St. Pierre, *John Steinbeck: The California Years* (San Francisco: Chronicle Books, 1983), p. 99.

9. Malcolm Cowley, *The New Republic* 98 (May 3, 1939): 383.

10. French, p. 109.

11. Edmund Wilson, *The Boys in the Back Room: Notes on California Novelists* (San Francisco: The Colt Press, 1941), pp. 42 and 49.

12. Howard Levant, *The Novels of John Steinbeck: A Critical Study* (Columbia, MO: University of Missouri Press, 1974), p. *ix*.

13. Ibid., p. 7.

14. Ibid., p. 128.

15. R. W. B. Lewis, "John Steinbeck: The Fitful Daemon" in *Steinbeck: A Collection of Critical Essays*, Robert Murray Davis, ed. (Englewood Cliffs, NJ: Prentice-Hall, 1972), p. 163.

16. *Steinbeck: A Life in Letters*, Elaine Steinbeck and Robert Wallsten, eds. (New York: Viking, 1975), p. 542. Subsequent references to this volume will be abbreviated as "L" and included as parenthetical numbers in the text.

17. St. Pierre, p. 112.

18. Louis Owens, *John Steinbeck's Re-Vision of America* (Athens, GA: University of Georgia Press, 1985), p. 5.

19. Wilson, p. 63.

20. Linda Ray Pratt, "Imagining Existence: Form and History in Steinbeck and Agee," *Southern Review* II (Winter 1975): 85 and 97.

21. Carol Shloss, *In Visible Light: Photography and the American Writer, 1840–1940* (New York: Oxford University Press, 1987), p. 217.

22. Joseph Millichap, *Steinbeck and Film* (New York: Ungar, 1983), p. 2.

23. Warren Motley, "From Patriarchy to Matriarchy: Ma Joad's Role in *The Grapes of Wrath*," *American Literature* 54 (October 1982): 405.

24. Letter to Mavis McIntosh, summer of 1941, in the *John Steinbeck Papers in the Clifton Waller Barrett Library of the University of Virginia*,

manuscript #6239-1, reprinted with permission of the Steinbeck estate.

25. Thomas Kiernan, *The Intricate Music: A Biography of John Steinbeck* (Boston: Little Brown, 1979), p. 229.

26. John Steinbeck, *The Long Valley* (New York: Viking, 1938; rpt. 1986), pp. 85–6. Subsequent references to pages in this volume will be abbreviated as "LV" and included as parenthetical numbers in the text.

27. John Steinbeck, *East of Eden* (New York: Viking, 1952), p. 1.

# 2

# Pilgrims' Politics: Steinbeck's Art of Conversion

STEPHEN RAILTON

*THE Grapes of Wrath* is a novel about things that grow – corn, peaches, cotton, and grapes of wrath. From the start Steinbeck identifies his vision of human history with organic, biological processes. A recurrent image is established in the first chapter, when the drought and wind in Oklahoma combine to uproot and topple the stalks of corn. In Chapter 29, the last of Steinbeck's wide-angle interchapters, it is the rain and flooding in California that "cut out the roots of cottonwoods and [bring] down the trees" (589). Tragically, even human lives are caught in this pattern of being pulled up from the soil. Farmers are made migrants. Forced to sell and burn all of their pasts that won't fit onto a homemade flatbed truck, they too are uprooted, torn from their identities. Right alongside this pattern, however, Steinbeck establishes a second one: that of seed being carried to new ground, new roots being put down. This image is announced in Chapter 3. The turtle who serves as the agent of movement in that chapter has attracted a lot of commentary from the novel's critics, but Steinbeck's main interest is not in the turtle. Chapter 3 is organized around seeds, all "possessed of the anlage of movement" (20). The turtle simply continues on its way, but by involuntarily carrying one "wild oat head" across the road, and accidentally dragging dirt over the "three spearhead seeds" that drop from it and stick in the ground (22), the mere movement of the turtle becomes part of the process of change and growth.

*The Grapes of Wrath* is a novel about an old system dying, and a new one beginning to take root. Movement, to Steinbeck, including the movement of history, works like the "West Wind" in Shelley's ode. It is "Destroyer and preserver" both; it scatters "the

27

leaves dead" and carries forward "The winged seeds." The system that is dying we can call American capitalism, the roots of which had always been the promises of individual opportunity and of private property as the reward for taking risks and working hard. Steinbeck makes it more difficult to name the new system that is emerging from the violent ferment of the old system's decay. It is certainly socialistic, yet a goal of the novel is to suggest that a socialized democracy is as quintessentially American as the individualistic dream it will replace. "Paine, Marx, Jefferson, Lenin" he writes in Chapter 14 (206) – this list would confound a historian, but it is meant to reassure the American reader by linking socialism with our own revolutionary tradition. That was one reason for his enthusiasm about the title his wife found for the novel. He wanted the whole of Julia Ward Howe's fighting song printed as a sort of preface, because, he wrote his editor at Viking,

> The fascist crowd will try to sabotage this book because it is revolutionary. They try to give it the communist angle. However, The Battle Hymn is American and intensely so. . . . So if both words and music are there the book is keyed into the American scene from the beginning. (L 174)

At the same time, by tying his novel of history to the rhythms and laws of nature, the growth of seeds, the fermenting of grapes, Steinbeck tries to suggest that this coming American revolution is inevitable, organically decreed. The western states sense "the beginning change" with the nervousness of "horses before a thunder storm" (204); on the road west, separate families "*grew to be* units of the camps" (265; my italics).

These repeated biological locutions allow the novelist to assume the role of a Darwinian prophet, reading the political future instead of the natural past. Revolution is made to seem as inexorably sure as evolution. The novel is simply recording the process. Yet this quasi-scientific stance, while it helps account for the authority with which Steinbeck's prose tells his story, belies the real engagement of the book. Critics have accused Steinbeck of being wrong, because the drastic social change he apparently predicted never took place. But he knew better than that. If he had himself believed the stance his narrative adopts, he would have written a much less brilliant book, for the novel owes its power to Steinbeck's urgent but painstaking intention to enact the revolution he apparently foresees. Even his assumption of change is part of his strategy for creating it. And Steinbeck knew what he was up against. Despite his desire to make his vision seem "American and intensely so," he undertakes the task of radically redefining the most fundamental values of American society. The novel uproots as much as the forces of either nature or capitalism do, though far more subtly. And, ultimately, there is hardly anything natural about the kind of change − "as in the whole universe only man can change" (267) − that Steinbeck is anxious to work. *Supernatural* probably describes it more accurately. Nor is *change* the right word for it, although it's the one Steinbeck regularly uses. *The Grapes of Wrath* is a novel about conversion.

You and I, the novel's readers, are the converts whom he is after. Working a profound revolution in our sensibilities is his rhetorical task. His chief narrative task, however, is to recount the story of the Joads' conversions. Thematically, Route 66 and the various state highways in California that the Joads travel along all run parallel to the road to Damascus that Saul takes in Acts, or to the Way taken by Bunyan's Christian in *Pilgrim's Progress*. The problem with the way most readers want to see that turtle in Chapter 3 as an emblem of the Joads is precisely that it denies their movement any inward significance. Steinbeck finds much to admire in the Joads and the class of "the people" whom they represent, including the fierce will to survive and keep going which they share with that turtle, but he explicitly makes the capacity for spiritual regeneration the essence of humanity. That humans can redefine the meaning of our lives is what makes us "unlike any other thing organic or inorganic in the universe" (204). Con-version − to turn around, to turn together −is a metaphysical movement. This is the route on which Steinbeck sets the Joads. For, as much as he finds to admire in them, he also knows that before American society can be saved from its sins, "the people" will have to change, too.

Thus there is a tension between the novel's rhetorical and its narrative tasks. Steinbeck is writing about the migrant families, not for them; their lives have no margin, either of income or leisure, for reading novels. He is writing for the vast middle class that forms the audience for best-selling fiction, and one of his goals is to educate those readers out of their prejudices against people like the Joads. As soon as they reach California, the Joads are confronted by the epithet "Okie," and the attitude that lies behind it: "'Them goddamn Okies got no sense and no feeling. They ain't human. . . . They ain't a hell of a lot better than gorillas'" (301). As victims of such prejudice, and of the economic exploitation that it serves to rationalize, the migrants are treated with nothing but respect by the novel. Steinbeck takes pains not to prettify their earthiness, but the whole book is a testimony to their immeasurable human worth. By bringing his readers inside the life of an "Okie" family, and keeping them there for so many hundreds of pages, Steinbeck writes as an advocate to the migrants' claims on America's understanding, compassion, and concern. That he does this largely by letting the Joads' lives and characters speak for themselves is one of the novel's great achievements.

As his letters from the winter of 1938 reveal, Steinbeck's decision to write the novel was precipitated by his own firsthand encounter with the thousands of dispossessed families who were starving in the valleys of California. At first he could only see the migrants as victims: "I want to put a tag of shame on the greedy bastards who are responsible for this" (L 161), by which he meant "the fascist group of utilities and banks and huge growers" (L 158). There is no mistaking the element of moral indignation in the novel he started that spring; although they never appear directly in it, the novel treats the large landowners as unequivocally, allegorically evil. But he had gotten beyond his first reaction to the plight of the migrants by deepening his insight into the causes of their exploitation. Although it can be misread as one, *The Grapes of Wrath* is not a morality play in which the virtues of the people contend with the viciousness of the "huge growers." The source of the economic injustices that drought and Depression magnified so drastically is in the values that the Joads themselves initially share with their oppressors in California.

Perhaps the truest thing about the novel is its refusal to sentimentalize the life in the Midwest from which the Joads and the other families they meet have been dispossessed. When their dream of a golden future out West is destroyed by the brutal realities of migrant life in California, the past they left at the other end

30

of Route 66 appeals to them as the paradise they have been driven from. When the novel winds up at the Hooper Ranch, the place seems as infernal as Simon Legree's plantation in *Uncle Tom's Cabin*. The armed guards, the filthy conditions, the edge of outright starvation on which Hooper Ranches, Inc., is content to keep the pickers — Steinbeck does want to expose this as one of the darkest places of the earth. At no point in the novel do the Joads feel further from "home," but Steinbeck also wants us to see how much Hooper's farm in California has in common with the Joad farm in Oklahoma that Tom had been trying to get back to at the beginning.

There is, for instance, a wire fence around both farms. The Joads didn't really need a fence, Tom tells Casy, but "'Pa kinda liked her there. Said it give him a feelin' that forty was forty'" (39). And Pa got the wire by taking advantage of his own brother. That is Steinbeck's point; that is what both fences delimit. We hear just enough about the Joads' earlier life in Oklahoma to recognize that they lived on their forty acres with essentially the same narrowly selfish values as Hooper on his much larger orchard. The Sooners took their land by force from the Indians, just as the large owners in California took theirs from the Mexicans. In both places, what prevailed was the "right" of the strongest — or say, the greediest. The Joads even stole the house they are evicted from. Grampa hangs onto the pillow he stole from Albert Rance with the same fierceness that the owners display in defense of their ill-gotten profits. Steinbeck's antagonist in the novel is not the group of large owners, but rather the idea of ownership itself. It is at the Hooper Ranch that Ma, on the verge of despair, grows most sentimental about the past:

> They was the time when we was on the lan'. They was a boundary to us then. Ol' folks died off, an' little fellas come, an' we was always one thing — we was the fambly — kinda whole and clear. (536)

Given what the Joads have been through since leaving home, it is impossible not to sympathize with her nostalgia. But finally, for Steinbeck, any kind of boundary — whether it's drawn around forty acres or forty thousand, around a family or a class — is wrong.

And it is "the quality of owning" that builds boundaries, that "freezes you forever into 'I,' and cuts you off forever from the 'we' " (206).

Yet if owning separates, dispossession becomes the basis for a new unity. If one set of values is being uprooted, that prepares the ground for another to develop. On the one hand, the westward journey of the Joads is a moving record of losses: their home and past, Grampa and Granma's deaths, Noah and Connie's desertions. The sufferings inflicted on the family bear witness not only to their strength of character, but also to the evils of the social and economic status quo. Their hapless pursuit of happiness indicts and exposes the America they move across. Steinbeck forces his reader to suffer even more steadily. Ma has a sudden moment of insight on the road west when she "seemed to know" that the family's great expectations were "all a dream" (225), but, for the first half of the novel at least, the Joads are sustained by their dreams. The reader is denied any such imaginative freedom. While most narratives are organized around some kind of suspense about what will happen next, *The Grapes of Wrath* is structured as a series of inevitabilities. Each of the book's wide-angle chapters precedes the Joads, and in them we see the tenant farmers being tractored off before Tom comes home to an empty house, or the new proletariat being exploited before the Joads even begin to look for work, or the rain flooding the migrant camps before the Joads try to battle the rising water. Again and again what will happen next is made narratively inescapable. "I've done my damndest to rip a reader's nerves to rags," Steinbeck wrote about the novel (L 178). It is a good technique for a protest novel. The narrative enacts its own kind of oppression, and, by arousing in its readers a desire to fight this sense of inevitability, it works strategically to arouse us toward action to change the status quo.

On the other hand, however, the journey of the Joads is also an inward one. And there the same pattern of losses is what converts their movement into a pilgrimage toward the prospect of a new consciousness. As in Bunyan's book, homelessness and suffering become the occasion of spiritual growth. In several of the interchapters Steinbeck describes this process: "The families, which had been units of which the boundaries were a house at night, a

32

farm by day, changed their boundaries" (267). They expand their boundaries. Having lost their land, the migrants' minds are no longer "bound with acres" (268); their new lives, their very losses, lead them toward the potentially redemptive discovery of their interrelatedness, their membership in a vastly extended family – the "we." In the novel's main narrative, Steinbeck dramatizes this process; near the very end, Ma sums up the new way she has learned to define her life: "'Use' ta be the fambly was fust. It ain't so now. It's anybody'" (606).

As an interpretive gloss on the meaning of her pilgrimage, however, Ma's pronouncement is much too pat. Simply quoting it denies Steinbeck the credit he deserves as both a novelist and a visionary. Again as in Bunyan's book, Steinbeck's faith is neither simple nor naive. Ruthie and Winfield, the youngest Joads, remind us how innately selfish human nature is. In his representation of their naked, nagging need for place and power, Steinbeck looks unflinchingly at the fact that "mine" is always among the first words an infant speaks. Similarly, Grampa and Granma are too old to learn to redefine themselves. The disruptions, the losses by which the others' assumptions are broken up, in the same way that a field has to be broken before new seed can be put into it, kill them both. Even with the other Joads, Steinbeck admits a lot of skepticism about whether they can be converted. Although Pa has become a victim of the capitalist system, it seems unlikely that he could ever abandon the economics of self-interest. As Tom tells Casy on the other side of the fence around the Hooper Ranch, it wouldn't do any good to tell Pa about the strike Casy is trying to organize: "'He'd say it wasn't none of his business. . . . Think Pa's gonna give up his meat on account a other fellas?'" (524).

Steinbeck here allows Tom, in his blunt vernacular voice, to ask the novel's most urgent question. The American Dream of individual opportunity has clearly betrayed "the people," but can they plant themselves on a different set of instincts? Can they redefine their boundaries? When he looks at the horrors of the migrants' plight, he knows that the answer is – They must. When he writes in the interchapters as an analyst of American society, the answer is – They will. But the narrative of the Joad family deals with specific people, not analytical abstractions. And their story, while it

33

leads to the birth of the new "Manself" that Steinbeck sees as the only hope for a failed nation, tells a different story. Its emphasis is on how long and hard, and finally private, is the labor by which that New Man will be delivered into the world. Shortly after beginning the novel, Steinbeck wrote his agent that "The new book is going well." But then he added, "Too fast. I'm having to hold it down. I don't want it to go so fast for fear the tempo will be fast and this is a plodding, crawling book" (L 167). One reason for the book's length is Steinbeck's appreciation of the almost insurmountable obstacles that lie on the path between "I" and "we." And time alone cannot accomplish the birth of a new sensibility. It will also require a kind of violence. As Casy replies to Tom in their exchange about Pa, "'I guess that's right. Have to take a beatin' 'fore he'll know'" (524). Even that turtle in Chapter 3 gets hit by a truck before the seeds it carries fall into the ground.

The threat of violence hangs over the land Steinbeck is surveying from the outset, when the evicted sharecroppers wonder whom they can shoot to save their farms. In Howe's hymn, of course, "the grapes of wrath" are immediately followed by that "terrible swift sword," and in those places where Steinbeck's prose rises to its most oratorical pitch, it seems to predict a second American civil war with all the righteousness of an Old Testament prophet: "three hundred thousand — if they ever move under a leader — the end. Three hundred thousand, hungry and miserable; if they ever know themselves, the land will be theirs and all the gas, all the rifles in the world won't stop them" (325). Yet such passages never ring quite true. They seem to be another of the rhetorical strategies by which Steinbeck is trying to work on the sensibilities of his readers: To their sympathy for the dispossessed he adds this appeal to their fear of what driven people might resort to. Organized, militant action is not at the center of Steinbeck's program for apocalyptic change. His concern is with consciousness. That is where the most meaningful revolution must occur. Even physical violence matters chiefly as a means to spiritual change.

It is because Steinbeck's emphasis is on inward experience that Jim Casy, a supernumerary as far as most of the book's action is concerned, is central to its plot. Casy's presence is what allows Steinbeck to dramatize his concern with consciousness. At the beginning, Steinbeck gives him a head start on the Joads. They are looking to start over in California; although they have lost their home and land, they still hang on to their belief in the American Dream. Casy, however, is looking to start anew. He has already lost the faith in the Christian values that had given meaning to his life, and is self-consciously questing for a new belief, a new cause to serve. He remains a preacher – long after he has rejected the title, the narrative continues to refer to him as "Reverend Jim Casy" and "the preacher" – but cannot find the Word he should announce. In much the same passivity as the novel's reader, he watches and absorbs the meaning of the Joad's attempt to carry their lives and ambitions westward. His first, indeed his only decisive action in the narrative itself is precipitated by an act of violence. In the Bakersfield Hooverville, a migrant named Floyd hits a deputy sheriff to avoid being arrested for the "crime" of telling the truth; when the deputy pulls his gun, Tom trips him; when he starts shooting recklessly into the camp, Casy knocks him out – it is worth noting the details because this same sequence will recur at the Hooper Ranch. In describing this action, Steinbeck's prose departs from its usual syntactic straightforwardness to signal its significance: "and then, suddenly, from the group of men, the Reverend Casy stepped" (361). His kicking the deputy in the neck is presented as an instinctual reflex, and his actions, here, and subsequently when he gives himself up to the deputy to save Floyd and Tom, speak a lot louder than any words he uses, but Reverend Casy has at last found a cause to serve.

That cause can be defined as the "group of men" he steps from, but it is also here that Casy disappears from the narrative for 150 pages. In this case Steinbeck refuses to allow his story to get ahead of itself. The exemplary significance of Casy's self-sacrifice is barely registered by the Joads, who still feel they have their own lives to live. And Casy himself cannot conceptualize the meaning of his involuntary action, or the values of the new faith he commits his life to, until later. When he reappears at the Hoover Ranch, he tries to explain it to Tom:

> "Here's me, been a-goin' into the wilderness like Jesus to try to find out somepin. Almost got her sometimes, too. But it's in the jail house I really got her." (521)

35

What he got in jail could be called an insight into the moral logic of socialism: that the greatest evil is human need, and that the only salvation lies in collective effort. Although the novel is deliberately vague about how Casy came to be at the Hooper Ranch, and what his role is in the strike there, we could see his new identity in strictly political terms: Like the strike organizers Steinbeck had written about in *In Dubious Battle,* Casy has committed himself to the cause of Communist revolution. As a fundamentalist preacher in Oklahoma, he had aroused and exhorted crowds to feel the operation of grace, and save their individual souls; as a left-wing strike organizer in California, he is teaching the migrants to organize and act in the interests of their class. But, at this crucial point, the novel complicates its message by keeping its focus on spiritual rather than political concerns. The individual soul retains its privileged position. For Casy's actions at the Hooper Ranch speak much less resonantly than his words, and the revolutionary change they bring about occurs inwardly.

Steinbeck brings Casy back into the narrative at this point to complete Tom Joad's conversion. Tom is the novel's central pilgrim. The book begins with his attempt to return "home." This works a nice inversion on *Pilgrim's Progress,* for Bunyan's Christian must choose to leave home before he can begin the path that leads to salvation. Tom has no choice; economic and natural forces have already exiled him from "home" before he can get there. In both works, however, the quest ultimately is for "home." For Bunyan, of course, the spirit's true home is in eternity, while all the action of Steinbeck's novel is set in this world. It is through this world that Tom moves to find a new home; it is still in this world that he finds it. But it is nonetheless a spiritual dwelling place that he finds. Tom chooses to leave his family at the end of his pilgrimage; almost the last thing he says before disappearing from the story is that Ma need not worry about where to find him:

> "Well, maybe like Casy says, a fella ain't got a soul of his own, but on'y a piece of a big one – an' then–"
> "Then what, Tom?"
> "Then it don't matter. Then I'll be all aroun' in the dark. I'll be ever'where – wherever you look." (572)

Wherever the people are – that is Tom's new home. All the boundaries around his self have dissolved. In this communion with the world soul, Tom finds a freedom that merely being paroled from prison could never provide, and a meaning that living for himself or for his family could never have bestowed upon his acts. By losing himself – to use the phrase that would have been equally familiar to Bunyan's readers and Casy's revivalist congregations – he has found himself.

As Tom's last conversation with Ma repeatedly acknowledges, Casy was the agent of his conversion. It is Casy's words ("like Casy says") and Casy's mystical presence ("Seems like I can see him sometimes" [572]) that show Tom the way that leads to his being's true home. But this conversion is only accomplished painfully, through another act of violence that indicates how much of Tom's old self must be destroyed before the exemplary New Man that he embodies can be born. Twice in Tom's last conversation with "the preacher," Casy asks him if he can't "see" the revelation that Casy has seen in the jail house, and that he is trying to realize at the Hooper Ranch. "No," Tom replies both times (521, 522), not because he is stupid, but because he has always lived within the boundaries of self-interest. As Casy had predicted about Pa, Tom, too, has to take a beating before he can know. Within a few minutes of this discussion, Tom is literally clubbed in the face. The more important "beating," however, occurs in the realm of Tom's spirit. In a scene that mirrors the moment of Casy's conversion at the Hooverville, Tom witnesses Casy's death at the hands of the "deputies" who have come to break the strike. It is out of the violent trauma of this act of witnessing that Tom's new self begins to emerge.

Steinbeck, using a club of his own, makes it impossible for the reader (who is also witnessing this violence) to overlook the scriptural power of Casy's life and death. His likenesses to Christ are established at the start, when a man with the initials "J. C." departs for California with twelve Joads. Not only does Casy die as a martyr: twice he tells the men who are about to kill him that they know not what they do (cf. 527). As if these cues were not enough, immediately after he dies one of the vigilantes says, "'Jesus, George. I think you killed him' " (527). And, as if even this were not enough, Ma has Tom repeat Casy's last words, then repeats them herself:

> "That's what he said – 'You don' know what you're doin' '?"
> "Yeah!"
> Ma said, "I wisht Granma could a heard." (535)

The most devoutly Christian of the Joads, Granma presumably would have taken the most pleasure from the preacher's appropriation of the Word. But, for all this, Steinbeck insists that we understand Casy's death and its implications in ways that Granma never could, unless she were willing to throw off her old self as well. For if it is easy to note how Christlike Casy is, especially in death, it is crucial to note how un-Christian, anti-Christian are the values to which his death converts Tom.

As others have noted, *The Grapes of Wrath* contains many echoes of and allusions to the Bible. Yet the novel never wavers on the point that Casy's rejection of Christianity makes at the very start. Throughout the book Steinbeck returns to Christianity only to attack it. He exposes and condemns the several "Jesus-lovers" whom the Joads meet, the Salvation Army as a Christian relief agency, the preachers who teach Christlike submission to Caesar. One of the ways that Ma is made to change in the course of her pilgrimage is by replacing her acquired faith in God and the next world with the belief in the people and in this life that she gradually learns from Casy. Who shall inherit the earth is among the book's most urgent questions, but Steinbeck has no patience with the idea that it shall be the meek. In his last talk with Ma, Tom's vernacular sums up the novel's displacement of Christianity, citing scripture to the end that Steinbeck has consistently had in mind:

> "most of the preachin' is about the poor we shall have always with us, an' if you got nothing', why, jus' fol' your hands an' to hell with it, you gonna git ice cream on gol' plates when you're dead. An' then this here Preacher says two get a better reward for their work." (571)

This "Preacher" is Solomon, whose words in Ecclesiastes Steinbeck converts into a socialist manifesto. Much like Melville in "The Try-Works" chapter of *Moby-Dick*, Steinbeck is using "unchristian Solomon's wisdom" to carry his readers beyond the New

Testament to a new revelation. Christianity itself is another evil that must be uprooted. And Casy's death not only completes his apotheosis by being paired with Christ's; it also violently repudiates the legacy of the Crucifixion. The strike breakers may not know what they're doing, but Casy doesn't ask anyone to forgive them for that reason. His death may be a martyrdom, but Tom's immediate, instinctive reaction to it is neither to love his enemies nor to turn the other cheek, but to murder the man who killed Casy.

It is surprising how little notice Tom's act of violence has gotten from the novel's commentators. In a sense, Tom's crime here is a more enlightened act than the murder he had gone to prison for before the novel begins. There he had killed to defend himself. Here he kills to avenge and defend an idea – the idea that Casy and the strike at Hooper's represent. His readiness to fight and kill for this larger concept is a measure of the spiritual distance he has traveled in the course of his pilgrimage. Like Casy's stepping forth at Bakersfield to knock out the deputy, Tom's involuntary action indicates his preparedness to take the final leap into the kingdom of spirit he attains at the end. But still, Tom's act is a brutal murder. He hits "George" four times in the head with a pick handle. Steinbeck hardly expected it to pass unnoticed. "Think I'll print a forward," he wrote about the novel, "warning sensitive people to let it alone" (L 168). He may even have been comparing himself as a writer to Tom's savage reaction when he added: "It pulls no punches at all and may get us all into trouble."

Once we have noticed all this, however, it is by no means easy to know what to make of it. While he was writing *The Grapes of Wrath,* Steinbeck apparently needed to disguise even from himself how skillfully the novel works to convert rather than confront the sensibilities of his audience. "I am sure it will not be a popular book" he wrote (L 172), not long before it zoomed to the top of the best-seller lists. He was writing a "revolutionary" novel fueled by his own wrath at the moral and economic horrors of contemporary America; such a work had to be "an outrageous book" (L 172). Yet his deeper need was to reach "the large numbers of readers" (L 172) he expected to outrage. His very ambitions as a prophet of social change depended on being read by the widest possible audience. His handling of Tom's murderous action epitomizes his own divided intentions. Tom's action aggressively defies the laws of both society and the New Testament. At the same time, Steinbeck makes it incredibly easy for his reader to accept Tom's act. Immediately afterward, he retreats to the shack on the ranch, and as soon as possible he confesses his crime to the whole family. When he and his mother are left alone, he goes over the event again, and Ma – who for 500 pages has stood for love and compassion – Ma unhesitatingly absolves him of any wrongdoing: "'I can't read no fault on you'" (535). By returning the "murderer" to the bosom of his family, and having him shriven by his own mother, Steinbeck domesticates his deed. In one respect, he disarms it of its radical power. In another, though, he uses it to further his task of radicalizing his audience's sensibilities: The reader who remains sympathetic to Tom has already been made, subliminally, an outlaw from the values of American society and the New Testament. Our willingness to harbor Tom, to continue to identify him as the book's moral hero, is a measure of *our* preparedness for conversion to a new vision of the truth.

We could explain Steinbeck's use of biblical typology along the same lines, as a purely rhetorical strategy. "Large numbers of readers" could not be expected to endorse militant socialism. Instead, Steinbeck shrewdly insinuates his revolutionary vision by presenting it in the familiar guise of Christianity. Just as Casy's quest carries him from the fundamentalist's Bible to a Marxist reading of Ecclesiastes, so Steinbeck's choice of Casy as the narrative agent of revelation allows the novel to find a middle ground between the conventional American's old allegiances and Steinbeck's newer testament. There would be nothing inherently wrong with such a device. Every novel of purpose must make some compromises with its audience if it wants to reach and move them. Yet explaining Steinbeck's affinity for the Bible this way would never get to the heart of his novel. His use of Christianity is more than strategic. For the private, inward operation of grace is as fundamental to his vision as it is to St. Paul's or Bunyan's.

To the doctrinaire socialist, meaning is found in collective action. Steinbeck offers his version of that ideal in his descriptions of the government camp at Weedpatch where the Joads stay for a month after being driven out of the Hooverville. The camp has a wire fence around it, too, but it only matters when the forces of capitalism try to destroy the communal harmony of the camp. The novel presents life in the camp as a Utopian but practicable antithesis to the selfishness that rules on both the Joad farm and the Hooper Ranch. In the camp happiness is pursued by owning things jointly, sharing responsibilities, making decisions by democratically elected committees. The camp's weekly square dances provide the book's most attractive image of a communal society: The music belongs to no one individual; the dancers obey the calls in unison and joy. It is not an accident that the Growers' Association and its hired reactionaries try to discredit the camp by disrupting a dance. That episode allows Steinbeck starkly to polarize the two worlds, within the camp and without: There's harmony and expression inside, violence and exploitation outside. He may in fact have meant for this portrayal of men and women acting collectively to occupy the center of the book's moral ground. But, if so, he complicates his own values by reintroducing Casy into the narrative, and shifting the drama back inside Tom's consciousness. He also betrays his misgivings about collective action as redemptive in the book's only other extended account of it. This occurs in the final chapter, when Pa convinces another group of migrants to work together to build a dam to save their campsites from the rising floodwater. Not only do their efforts fail; although they work frantically through the night with as much unison as those square dancers, their shared labor brings them no closer to true unity, no nearer to the "we," than they had been before. To recognize and act collectively in the interests of the group, it seems, is not enough. Indeed, since the men remain divided and bitter after the failure of their dam, it seems that collective action in itself is meaningless.

Instead, what the novel presents as most meaningful are Casy's and Tom's conversions: the purpose and inner peace that each man finds, not in acting with others, but in "feeling" or "seeing" his oneness with all. Casy, presumably, is acting at Hooper's to organize the strike – but it is telling that the novel has no interest in elaborating such a role. Tom at the end does tell Ma what he aims to *do:* "'What Casy done,' he said" (571) – but again, what that means is left extremely vague, although Tom goes on to talk in eloquent detail about what he will *be* as the disembodied spirit of the people. The novel's two most important events, if we can call them events, actually occur in private – to Casy in jail, and to Tom while he's hiding out after killing the vigilante. Still more striking is the fact that both these "events" occur entirely outside the narrative. It is offstage, in solitude, alone with his own consciousness that each man somehow arrives at the new faith that Steinbeck is preaching to us, becomes the New Man who can redeem the waste land. Thus Steinbeck offers an essentially religious and mystical solution to the economic and political problems that inspired him to write the novel in the first place. For when we compare the rapturous accents of Tom's last speech with Ma to Pa's futile efforts to organize the migrants to battle circumstances together, we're left with the conclusion that people merely working together cannot succeed – while one person who has experienced unity with the "big soul," whatever he or she does, cannot fail. Despite the narrative's persistent attention to external forces – natural, historical, economic, social – it ultimately points to what its own representation excludes, to an inward "act" of consciousness or spirit, as the only place the revolution can begin. And once Tom has been brought "home" to this sense of selflessness, it seems that the revolution is effectively over as well.

Of course, Tom's climactic scene with Ma, although it does bring the novel's central pilgrimage into Steinbeck's version of the Celestial City, is not the end of the story. Tom's apotheosis is followed by two additional moments of conversion, both of which are brought on by another kind of violence: the death in birth of the baby that Rose of Sharon has been carrying through the novel. Death in birth, in keeping with the pattern of uprooting and planting, destruction and new growth, leads to birth out of death. The first conversion is Uncle John's, and it occurs when he goes out into the rain to bury the stillborn infant. Up until this moment, John has been crippled by the guilt he has felt since his wife's death many years ago. But now, having been pushed around by the American economic system and knocked down by the floodwaters, John reaches a higher state of consciousness. With the wrath of an

42

inspired Biblical prophet, he sends the dead baby down the flood as a judgment and curse on the society that produced it. In the swirling waters he has been cleansed of more than his guilt; he's been freed entirely from his fundamentalist Christian's sense of sinfulness; he's been politically radicalized. It is not he who is damned, but the nation.

Like Tom's unforgiving reaction to Casy's death, John's conversion from guilt to wrath is Steinbeck's way of insisting that his faith is a newer testament. To be saved, the nation needs to be converted, yet it will have to leave Christianity as well as capitalism behind. The novel's very last scene tries to build a bridge between the realm of spirit, where individuals find their home, and the world of action, where men and women can help each other; it redresses the imbalance of Tom's story, where the emphasis had been almost entirely on faith, by adding to that a doctrine of works. Thematically, the novel's last scene is perfect. It is the moment of Rose of Sharon's conversion. Out of the violent loss of her baby (which she has "witnessed" with her whole body) comes a new, self-less sense of self. When she breastfeeds the starving stranger who would otherwise die, a new, boundary-less definition of family is born. Rose of Sharon's act is devoutly socialistic: from each according to ability, to each according to need. At the same time, the novel's last word on this scene, which is also the novel's last word, is "mysteriously" — a word that has no place in Marx's or Lenin's vocabulary. The scene's implications are as much religious as political. Iconographically, like Casy's death, this tableau of a man lying in a woman's lap both recalls and subverts the familiar imagery of Christianity. By calling our ultimate act of attention in the novel to the look of "mysterious" satisfaction on Rose of Sharon's face, Steinbeck keeps this scene in line with his focus on the private, inward, ineffable moment of conversion. Yet here we also see how that inner change can lead to redemptive action. The barn in which this scene takes place is not only "away in a manger"; it is also halfway between the social but bureaucratic world of the government camp and the spiritual but solitary state that Tom found while hiding out in the bushes. And what happens in this barn triumphantly completes the novel's most pervasive pattern:

One family has been uprooted and destroyed; out of those ruins, another, a new one, takes root. Manself can change, and by change can triumph over the most devastating circumstances.

For all its thematic aptness, however, this ending has been widely condemned. I can certainly understand why adolescent readers, especially young women, are uncomfortable with the picture of a teenage girl suckling a middle-aged, anonymous man. We can see Steinbeck's divided attitude toward his readers at work in this scene too: He gives them an ending that is essentially happy, but also disturbing. I frankly find it harder to see why adult critics have singled out this particular scene to object to. Rose of Sharon's conversion does not occur more suddenly than Tom's or John's – or, for that matter, than Saul's on the road to Damascus. The scene is unquestionably sentimental, but Steinbeck's most dramatic effects are invariably melodramatic – Ma sitting with Granma's corpse across the desert, Casy's death, Tom's valedictory eloquence, the anathema John pronounces with a dead baby in his arms. The novel could hardly have the impact it does on most readers without these unlikely, outsized gestures. For that matter, almost all novels of protest try to pluck the reader's heartstrings, and homelessness and hunger in a land of plenty is an inarguably legitimate cause in which to appeal to people's emotions. Steinbeck's editors at Viking were the first readers to object to the ending. Refusing to change a word of it, he defended it on the grounds of "balance" (L 178). I find it a strange but powerful tribute to Steinbeck's faith in selflessness as the one means by which men and women can transcend their circumstances in a world that is otherwise so harshly and unjustly determined. I think it would be less powerful if it were any less strange.

In any case, whether the novel's last scene is esthetically successfuly is probably not the most important question to ask. Having seen the starving migrants in the valleys of California, and determined to write a novel in response to that human fact, Steinbeck was shocked out of his modern assumption that art mattered more than life. At the end of a letter from the winter of 1938, recording in horrified detail his own reaction as a witness to the sufferings of the migrant families, he wrote: "Funny how mean and little books become in the face of such tragedies" (L 159). He wrote the novel in the belief to which the trauma of seeing the homeless, wretched families had converted him: that American society had to change, quickly and profoundly. This then leads to the largest question raised by the novel's several endings. Is conversion the same as revolution? Can the re-creation of society be achieved by an individual's private, inner, spiritual redefinition of the self?

That Steinbeck believed it could is the most "intensely American" aspect of the novel. "Paine, Marx, Jefferson, Lenin" – those names are relevant to his vision, but the tradition to which *The Grapes of Wrath* belongs is best identified with a different list: Winthrop, Edwards, Emerson, Whitman. Steinbeck's emphasis on inner change as the basis of social salvation has its roots in the Puritan belief that the New Jerusalem is identical with the congregation of converted saints, and in the Transcendentalists' credo that, as Emerson put it, "The problem of restoring to the world original and eternal beauty is solved by the redemption of the soul." Harriet Beecher Stowe, as the author of *Uncle Tom's Cabin*, has to occupy an especially prominent place on that list. Her great protest novel is also organized around movement as both a means to expose social evil and as the pilgrimage of the spirit toward home. And when Stowe, in her last chapter, sought to answer the many aroused readers who had written to ask her what they could *do* to solve the terrible problem of slavery, her response was, "they can see to it that *they feel right.*" It is in this ground that the seeds of Steinbeck's revolution must also grow. Tom and Rose of Sharon at last feel right when they have redefined themselves as one with the people around them. Steinbeck oppresses and exhorts, threatens and inspires, shocks and moves us to bring us each, individually, to the same point of communion.

Ultimately, of course, people's feelings are all that any novelist has to work with. Even if Steinbeck had gone on to specify exactly what Tom will do to realize the vision of human unity that he has attained, Tom could never act in the real world. He can only act on the reader, as Casy's example acted on him. Hiding out in the bushes or reading *The Grapes of Wrath* both occur in private. Any change that the novel might make in American society will have to happen first in the consciousness of its readers. But this doesn't

answer the question raised by Steinbeck's politics of consciousness. The origins of the evils that the novel decries are, as many of
the interchapters insist, social and economic. They result from
patterns of ownership, margins of profit, lack of security, and the
other characteristics of a capitalistic system with a dispossessed
proletariat to exploit. Can anything but a social revolution change
that system? *Pilgrim's Progress,* like the sermons Casy preached
before losing his original faith, is about getting to heaven; that
kind of salvation depends upon inner change. But Steinbeck wants
to save the nation from its sins. Babies like Rose of Sharon's are
dying because of social inequalities and economic injustices. Can
the private, spiritual birth of a New Man or a New Woman – the
unrecorded "event" that the novel leaves at the center of its narrative and its vision – affect that?

# 3

# "Happy[?]-Wife-and-Motherdom"[1]: The Portrayal of Ma Joad in John Steinbeck's *The Grapes of Wrath*

NELLIE Y. MCKAY

WOMEN'S social roles in western culture are central concerns in contemporary feminist criticism. The discourse focuses on the idea that our society is organized around male-dominated sex–gender systems that admit two genders, that privilege heterosexual relationships, and that embrace a sexual division of labor in which wife and mother are the primary functions of women.[2] In such works as *Of Woman Born* by Adrienne Rich,[3] *Man's World, Woman's Place* by Elizabeth Janeway,[4] *The Reproduction of Motherhood: Psychoanalysis and the Sociology of Gender* by Nancy Chodorow,[5] and *Contemporary Feminist Thought* by Hester Eisenstein,[6] critics argue that, in spite of prevailing social dogma to the contrary, the biological functions of childbearing and lactation (motherhood), and the cultural one of nurturing (mothering) are divisible. Whereas one is restricted to women, the other need not be. Parenting, in place of mothering, is not biologically determined, and there is no proof that men are less capable of nurturing children than women, or that children would suffer adverse effects if women were not their primary caretakers. However, female oppression under patriarchy dictates an institution in which the heterosexual family is at the center of the social system; woman, wife, motherhood, and mothering are synonymous; and sex-role stereotyping separates the social expectations of women from those of men. From this institution, "Happy-Wife-and-Motherdom" assumes woman's ideal social, emotional, and psychological state.

The success of such sex-role stereotyping depends on establishing socially acceptable clusters of behavioral attitudes that define male and female gender identities differently from the biological (sex-based) identities of women and men. To function properly,

47

these behaviors require social placement on a hierarchical scale of dominant versus submissive, strong versus weak, independent versus dependent, in favor of men.[7] Consequently, women are conditioned toward passivity while men are rewarded for more aggressive behavior. For women, the expressive traits (affection, obedience, sympathy, and nurturing) are hailed and rewarded as "normal" behavior; men are expected to be aggressive, tenacious, ambitious, and responsible. Objecting to psychological impositions that render women subordinate to men, Elizabeth Janeway, among others, speaks out against social scientists like Freud and Eric Erickson who, in defense of the status quo, made it their business to substitute *"prescription"* for *"description,"* as they tried to explain how women ought to be, rather than how they are.[8] She argues that there is no scientific basis for the male-constructed definition of women's nature, and that opinions on the biological aspects of women's inabilities to perform as well as men in some areas, and vice versa, are not facts, but are, rather, social mythology based on beliefs and practices that shape social life according to a particular set of values.[9] This social mythology of women's nature enables men to define the "natural" capabilities of women in ways that make women socially and economically dependent on men.

The image of woman/wife/mother with children as the "core of domestic organization is implicit in patriarchal sex–gender systems."[10] Traditionally, men perform in the public sphere, while women's place is in the home, where they loom large and powerful, although, in the larger world, they remain under the control of husbands and fathers. Nor are women innocent in the development of these systems. Several feminist critics now argue that sex-role differentiation originated partly in male propaganda, and partly because women found certain of its elements sufficiently attractive willingly to give up intellectual, economic, and political power in exchange for private power in the domestic sphere. As women/wives/mothers, they are able to hold sway over the lives of their children, and to manipulate their husbands in the sexual arena.[11] This arrangement frees men from domestic responsibilities and permits them to focus their lives primarily in the public sphere: the masculine world of social and political control that determines the lives of men and women. The husband/father assumes the socially approved masculine responsibility to make important decisions and provide monetarily for his family, while the wife/mother agrees to accept a variety of unspecified familial obligations, including constant attunement to the needs of her husband and children. His support is expected to be largely material; hers, emotional. Nor are the rewards equal. By society's standards, his contributions to the family are perceived greater; hers are lesser. He articulates his family and gives it a place in the larger world; she is bound by that articulation.[12]

Until recently, literary representations of women, especially by men, subscribed almost exclusively to the ideology of locating women's place in the domestic world. Women who moved outside of their designated boundaries in search of authority over their own lives were stigmatized as unfeminine, bad mothers and wives, and social deviants. The most well-known positive image in the category of the good woman is the Earth Mother, who, engaged in selfless mothering, dedicates her entire being to the welfare of her husband and children. In *The Lay of the Land,* Annette Kolodny reminds us of how powerful the representation of a symbiotic relationship between femaleness and the land (the earth) is in the national consciousness. The desire for harmony between "man" and nature, based on an experience of the land as woman/mother – the female principle of "receptivity, repose, and integral satisfaction," is one of our most cherished American fantasies, she tells us.[13] In her analysis of seventeenth- and eighteenth-century writings by early settlers in America, Kolodny writes that the members of this group carried with them a yearning for paradise, and perceived the New World as a "maternal 'garden,' receiving and nurturing human children."[14] Furthermore, she asserts that for these settlers there was

> a *need* to experience the land as a nurturing, giving maternal breast. . . . Beautiful, indeed, that wilderness appeared – but also dark, uncharted, and prowled by howling beasts. . . . Mother was ready to civilize it . . . [to make] the American continent . . . the birthplace of a new culture . . . with new and improved human possibilities . . . in fact as well as metaphor, a womb of generation and a provider of sustenance.[15]

49

This equation of the American land with woman's biological attributes did much to foster the widespread use of literary images of women as one with the "natural" propensities of a productive nurturing earth, and to erase, psychologically, the differences between the biological and the social functions of women.

Fully immersed in this tradition, men, male vision, and the relationships of men to each other and to the rest of the world dominate the works of John Steinbeck, whereas women, without whom the men would have no world, have no independent identity of their own. The social and economic conditions in the lower working-class milieu in which many of these women appear can easily give rise to what on the surface seems to represent a very different relationship to the social structure from that of women in other strata. On the contrary, the ideology that woman's place is rooted in her interests in others, preferably those of husbands and children, remains the same. Steinbeck's women seldom need seek the right to work outside of their homes, or to choose careers equal to those of men. They have no connections to the "gentle-companions" female identity or to the ideology of femininity that became popular in the nineteenth century. Work, as hard as that of farm men, or lower class men struggling for survival outside of the agrarian economy, occupies a great deal of their time. In the words of Tom Joad, "Women's always tar'd, . . . that's just the way women is, 'cept at meetin' once an' again."[16] They are always tired because they are always attending to the needs of everyone but themselves. Even domestic violence against these women is socially acceptable within the group.[17] Only race privilege protects them from the barbarous abuse of others outside of their community that women of color in similar situations experience. Yet, the most they can achieve and hold onto with social dignity is the supportive nurturing role of woman's place in a man's world.

The centrality of women to the action of *The Grapes of Wrath* is clear from the beginning as well. For one thing, not only among the Joads, the main characters in this novel, but in all the families in crisis, the children look to the women for answers to their immediate survival: "What are we going to do, Ma? Where are we going to go?" (47) the anonymous children ask. In male-dominated sex-gender systems, children depend on their mothers for parenting, and their stability rests mainly on the consistency and reliability with which women meet their needs. There is no question that in this model the woman/wife/mother makes the most important contributions to family stability. This chapter does not challenge Steinbeck's understanding of the value of women's roles in the existing social order. I attempt, however, to place his vision of those roles within the framework of an American consciousness that has long been nourished by gender myths that associated women with nature, and thus primarily with the biological and cultural functions of motherhood and mothering, whereas men occupy a separate masculine space that affords them independence and autonomy. By adopting Robert Briffault's theory that matriarchy is a cohesive, nonsexually dominating system,[18] Steinbeck assures us that the family can survive by returning to an earlier stage of collective, nonauthoritarian security while the larger society moves toward a socialistic economy. As he sees it, in times of grave familial or community need, a strong, wise woman like Ma Joad has the opportunity (or perhaps the duty) to assert herself and still maintain her role as selfless nurturer of the group. In this respect, she is leader and follower, wise and ignorant, and simple and complex, simultaneously.[19] In short, she is the woman for all seasons, the nonintrusive, indestructible "citadel" on whom everyone else can depend.

This idealistic view of womanhood is especially interesting because, although there are qualities in Steinbeck's work that identify him with the sentimental and romantic traditions, as a writer with sympathies toward socialism he also saw many aspects of American life in the light of harsh realism. His reaction to the plight of the Oklahoma farmers in this novel moved him to a dramatic revision of the frontier patriarchal myth of individual, white-male success through unlimited access to America's abundant and inexhaustible expanses of land. He begins with the equivalent of a wide-lens camera view that portrays the once-lush land grown tired and almost unyielding from overuse, and then follows that up with vivid descriptions of farmers being brutally dispossessed by capitalist greed from the place they thought belonged to them. His instincts are also keen in the matter of character development; unanticipated circumstances alter the worldview that many of the people in the novel previously held, and their changes are logical. As they suffer, the Joads, in particular the mother and her son Tom (the other Joad men never develop as fully), gradually shed their naïveté and achieve a sound political consciousness of class and economic oppression. This is a difficult education for them, but one which they eventually accept. Through it all, without the unshakable strength and wisdom of the mother, who must at times assert her will to fill the vacuum of her husband's incapability, nothing of the family, as they define it, would survive. Still, she never achieves an identity of her own, or recognizes the political reality of women's roles within a male-dominated system. She is never an individual in her own right. Even when she becomes fully aware of class discrimination and understands that the boundaries of the biological family are much too narrow a structure from which to challenge the system they struggle against, she continues to fill the social space of the invincible woman/wife/mother.

Critics identify two distinct narrative views of women in Steinbeck's writings. In one, in novels such as *To a God Unknown* (1933) and *The Grapes of Wrath* (1939), the image is positive and one-dimensional, with female significance almost completely associated with the maternal roles that Kolodny and others decry. In the other, for example *Tortilla Flat* (1935), *Of Mice and Men* (1937), *East of Eden* (1952), and several of the short stories in *The Long Valley* (1938), the portraiture is socially negative. Whores, hustlers, tramps, or madams are the outstanding roles that define the majority of these women. More graphically stated by one critic, these women "seem compelled to choose between homemaking and whoredom."[20] Interestingly, in spite of their questionable behavior, women within this group are often described as "big-breasted, big-hipped, and warm," thus implying the maternal types.[21] In his post-1943 fiction, after he moved to New York City, sophisticated women characters who are jealous, vain, and cunning – the opposite of the women in his earlier works – appear (as negative portrayals) in Steinbeck's work. Furthermore, Steinbeck's "positive" women are impressively "enduring," but never in their own self-interests. Their value resides in the manner in which they are able to sustain their nurturing and reproductive capabilities for the benefit of the group. As Mimi Reisel Gladstein notes,

52

they act as the nurturing and reproductive machinery of the group. Their optimistic significance lies, not in their individual spiritual triumph, but in their function as perpetuators of the species. They are not judged by any biblical or traditional sense of morality.[22]

In conjunction with their ability to endure and to perpetuate the species, they are also the bearers of "knowledge – both of their husbands and of men generally," knowledge which enables them to "come . . . [closer than men] to an understanding of the intricacies of human nature and the profundities of life in general."[23]

Since its publication in 1939, *The Grapes of Wrath*, one of Steinbeck's most celebrated works, has been the subject of a variety of controversial appraisals. Seen by some as "an attempted prose epic, a summation of national experience at a given time,"[24] others belabor its ideological and technical flaws. The disagreements it continues to raise speak well for the need to continue to evaluate its many structural and thematic strands.

The novel opens on a note that explodes the American pastoral of the seventeenth and eighteenth centuries that Kolodny describes in her work. The lush and fertile lands that explorers in Virginia and the Carolinas saw give way to the Oklahoma Dust Bowl, where ". . . dawn came, but no day. In the gray sky a red sun appeared, a dim red circle that gave a little light, like dusk; and as that day advanced, the dusk slipped toward darkness, and the wind cried and whimpered over the fallen corn" (5). The impotence and confusion of a bewildered group of displaced people replace the assuredness and confidence of the nation's early settlers. In this world where nature is gone awry, and human control lies in the hands of men greedy for wealth and in possession of new technology that enhances their advantages, the men, women, and children who have, until now, lived on the land are helpless against an unspeakable chaos.

Feeling completely out of control in a situation they cannot comprehend, the men stand in silence by their fences or sit in the doorways of the houses they will soon leave, space that echoes loudly with their impotent unspoken rage, for they are without power or influence to determine their destinies. Even more outrageous for them is their profound sense of alienation. Armed with rifles, and willing to fight for what they consider rightfully theirs, there is no one for them to take action against. They can only stare helplessly at the machines that demolish their way of life. They do not understand why they no longer have social value outside of their disintegrating group, and they do not know how to measure human worth in terms of abstract economic principles. "One man on a tractor can take the place of twelve or fourteen families," the representatives of the owner men explain to the uncomprehending displaced farmers. That some of their own people assist the invaders leaves them more befuddled.

> "What are you doing this kind of work for —against your own people?"

a farmer asks the tractor-driver son of an old acquaintance. The man replies:

> [for] "three dollars a day. . . . I got a wife and kids. We got to eat. . . . and it comes everyday."
> "But for three dollars a day fifteen or twenty families can't eat at all,"

the farmer rebuts, and continues:

> "nearly a hundred people have to go out and wander on the roads for your three dollars a day. Is that right?" . . . And the driver says, "Can't think of that. Got to think of my own kids. Three dollars a day, and it comes in every day. Times are changing, mister, don't you know? Can't make a living on the land unless you've got two, five, ten thousand acres and a tractor. Crop land isn't for little guys like us anymore. . . . You try to get three dollars a day some place. That's the only way." (50)

The quality of the frustration and level of the ineffectiveness that the men feel is displayed in the actions of Grampa, the patriarch of the Joad clan. He fires a futile shot at the advancing tractor, but succeeds only in "blow[ing] the headlights off that cat', . . . [while] she come on just the same" (62). The march of technology and the small farmers' distress go hand in hand.

Deprived of traditional assertive masculine roles, for the most part, the helpless, silent men seldom move; only their hands are engaged — uselessly — "busy," with sticks and little rocks as they survey the ruined crops, their ruined homes, their ruined way of life, "thinking – figuring," and finding no solution to the disintegration rapidly enveloping them. Nor do the women/ wives/mothers precipitously intrude on their shame. They are wise in the ways of mothering their men; of understanding the depth of their hurt and confusion, and in knowing that at times their greatest contribution to the healing of the others' psychic wounds lies in their supportive silence. "They knew that a man so hurt and so perplexed may turn in anger, even on people he loves. They left the men alone to figure and to wonder in the dust" (7). Secretly, unobtrusively, because they are good women, they study the faces of their men to know if this time they would "break." Also furtively, the children watch the faces of the men and the women. When the men's faces changed from "bemused perplexity" to anger and resistance, although they still did not know what they would do, the women and children knew they were "safe" – for "no misfortune was too great to bear if their men were whole" (7).

In the face of such disaster, enforced idleness is the lot of men. Their work comes to a halt. The women, however, remain busy, for the housewife's traditional work, from which society claims she derives energy, purpose, and fulfillment, goes on. In addition, as conditions worsen and the men further internalize impotence, the women know they will be responsible for making the crucial decisions to lead their families through the adjustment period ahead. Critic Joan Hedrick explains the dynamics of the division of labor in sex-gender-differentiated systems this way, rather than as women's "nature":

> Though there are no crops to be harvested, there are clothes to mend, cornmeal to stir, side-meat to cut up for dinner. In a time of unemployment, women embody continuity, not out of some mythic identity as the Great Mother, but simply because their work, being in the private sphere of the family, has not been taken away. . . .[25]

According to critics Richard Astro and Warren Motley, Steinbeck's philosophy of women was deeply influenced by his readings of Robert Briffault's *The Mothers: The Matriarchal Theory of Social Origins* (1931), a work they include in a group that "strove to heal the . . . post-Darwinian split between scientific thinking and ethical experience."[26] Although Briffault saw matriarchy (historically antecedent to patriarchy) as a primitive and regressive order, he felt it described a "relationship based on cooperation rather than power," and fostered an "equalitarian" society to which "authority" and "domination" were foreign. As Motley sees it, Steinbeck did not believe that matriarchy was regressive, but he was convinced that the shock of dispossession undermined the patriarchal authority (based on male economic dominance) of the Joad men and the other farmers to such an extent that they were forced to turn back to matriarchy, the more positive social organization force, epitomized by Ma Joad's "high calm," "superhuman understanding," and selfless concern for her family, as the hope for a better future.[27] Matriarchy, divested of the threat of authority and domination over men, was a system that suited Steinbeck's purpose in this novel.

*The Grapes of Wrath* delineates the tragedy of an agrarian family in a world in which capitalist greed and the demands of rapidly advancing technology supercede human needs and extenuating financial circumstances. Different in their attitudes from other white groups who seek the American Dream in social and economic mobility, the hard-working Joads, once tenant farmers, now reduced to share-cropper status, lived contentedly on the land in a community of like others, for three generations. They asked little of anyone outside of their world. Solid Americans, as they understand that term, they wanted only to live and let live. For instance, oblivious to the implications of his racial politics, the tenant man proudly explains his family's contributions to the pioneer history of white America. His grandfather arrived in frontier Oklahoma territory in his youth, when his worldly possessions amounted to salt, pepper, and a rifle. But before long, he successfully staked out a claim for his progeny:

> Grampa took up the land, and he had to kill the Indians and drive them away. And Pa was born here, and he killed weeds and snakes. . . . An we [the third succeeding generation] was born here. . . . And Pa had to borrow money. The bank owned the land then, but we stayed and got a little bit of what we raised. (45)

Unfortunately, the irony of their helplessness in confrontation with the power of the banks, with the absent, large land owners, and with the great crawling machines versus the fate of the Indians (to the farmer, of no greater concern than the comparison he makes of them to snakes or weeds) completely escapes the present generation. The subsequent education in class politics might have come sooner and been less psychologically devastating to the Joads and their friends if they had been able to recognize the parallels between racial and economic hegemony.

Three characters drive the action in *The Grapes of Wrath:* Jim Casy, a country preacher turned political activist; Tom Joad, the eldest son, ex-convict, and moral conscience of the family; and the indestructible Ma Joad, who holds center stage. At times she assumes mythic proportions, but her portraiture is also realistic and she acts with wisdom. Impressionistically, she is firmly planted in the earth, but she is more dependable than the land, which could not withstand the buffeting of nature or the persistent demands of small farmers or the evil encroachment of technology and corporate power. Her position is established at the beginning of the novel:

> Ma was heavy, but not fat; thick with child-bearing and work. . . . her strong bare feet moved quickly and deftly over the floor. . . . Her full face was not soft; it was controlled, kindly. *Her hazel eyes seemed to have experienced all possible tragedy and to have mounted pain and suffering like steps into a big calm and superhuman understanding. She seemed to know, to accept, to welcome her position, the citadel of the family.* (99–100 – italics mine)

Unless she admitted hurt or fear or joy, the family did not know those emotions; and better than joy they loved her calm. They could depend on her "imperturbability." When Tom, Jr., returns from prison to find no homestead, the house pushed off its foundations, fences gone, and other signs of living vanished, his first thought is "They're gone – or Ma's dead" (56). He knows that under no circumstances would she permit the place to fall into such ruin if she were there. His is not a casual observation, but a statement fraught with anxiety. As Nancy Chodorow points out, in the sex–gender system, the absent mother is always the source of discomfiture for her children. Tom Joad closely associates the physical deterioration of his home with a missing mother, a signal for him of the catastrophe of which he is yet unaware.[28]

There is no question that Steinbeck had, as Howard Levant stresses, "profound respect" and "serious intentions" for the materials in *The Grapes of Wrath*. His sympathies are with a group of people who, though politically and economically unaggressive by other traditional American standards, represented an important core in the national life.[29] His portrayal of the misfortunes and downfall of this family constitutes a severe critique of a modern economic system that not only devalues human lives on the basis of class but, in so doing, that violates the principles of the relationship between hard work and reward and the sanctity of white family life on which the country was founded. In light of the brutal social and economic changes, and the disruptions of white family stability, there is no doubt that Steinbeck saw strong women from traditional working-class backgrounds as instrumental in a more humane transformation of the social structure. Of necessity, women are essential to any novel in which the conventional family plays a significant role. Here, he gives the same significance to the destruction of a family-centered way of life that one group had shaped and perpetrated for generations as he does to the economic factors that precipitated such a dire situation. Furthermore, through female characters in *The Grapes of Wrath*, Steinbeck's sensitivities to the values of female sensibilities demonstrate a point of view that supports the idea of humanitarian, large-scale changes that would make America, as a nation, more responsive to larger social needs.

In this respect, in spite of the grim reality of the lives of the Joads and their neighbors, *The Grapes of Wrath* is optimistic in favor of massive social change. We can trace this optimism from the beginning of the book, in which, unlike traditional plots of the naturalistic novels of its day, events unfold through the consciousness of the characters in such a way as to permit them to envision themselves exercizing free will and exerting influence on their social world. In addition, as a result of his economic politics, Steinbeck reinforces the idea that the situation is not the dilemma of an isolated family, but of an entire group of people of a particular class. If sufficiently politicized, they can and will act. The novel chronicles the misfortunes and political education of the Joad family, but they represent the group from which they come, and share the feelings of their like-others. For example, also at the beginning, an unnamed farmer, recognizing his individual impotence in the face of capitalism and the technological monster, protests: "We've got a bad thing made by man, and by God that's something *we* can change" (52 – italics mine). While neither he nor his fellow farmers can comprehend the full meaning of that statement at the time, the end of the novel suggests that those who survive will come to realize that group action can have an effect on the monstrous ideology that threatens their existence. But first they must survive; and the women are at the center of making that survival possible.

The first mention of Ma Joad in the novel occurs when Tom, recently released from jail after serving four of a seven-year sentence for killing a man in self-defense, returns to the homestead to find it in ruin. During his absence, he had almost no contact with his family, for, as Tom observes to his friend Casy: "they wasn't people to write" (57). Two years earlier, however, his mother sent him a Christmas card, and, the following year, the grandmother did the same. His mother's appears to have been appropriate; his grandmother's, a card with a "tree an' shiny stuff [that] looks like snow," with an embarrassing message in "po'try," was not:

> Merry Christmus, purty child,
> Jesus meek an' Jesus mild,
> Underneath the Christmus tree
> There's a gif' for you from me. (35)

Tom recalls the teasing of his cellmates who saw the card. Subsequently, they call him "Jesus Meek."

Given the living situation within the Joad community – the hard work and frustration over the yield of the land and the absence of genteel rituals, especially in such hard times – the fact that both women sent Christmas cards to the incarcerated young man is testimony to the quality of their commitment to mothering. Granma's card, however, is not appropriate for the young man confined involuntarily among men for whom only masculine symbols and behavior are acceptable. Nevertheless, Tom does not hold this against her. He understands and accepts her impulse and her motive. He believes she liked the card for its shiny exterior and that she never read the message, perhaps because, having lost her glasses several years before, she could not see to read. Symbolically, Granma may have good intentions, but she lacks the perception to fill successfully the present or future needs of her family. Later, when both grandparents die enroute to California, the family realizes that they were too old to make the transition from one way of life to another. On the other hand, although there is no mention of the nature of Ma Joad's card, we can assume that it was not a cause of embarrassment for her son. She is the woman of wisdom who knows how to use her talents to comfort her family in its moments of greatest distress. The differences in the two Christmas cards set the stage for understanding that Ma Joad is the woman who will be the significant force in the life of the family in the difficult times ahead.

Critics of Steinbeck's women often note that the first time we come face to face with Ma Joad she is engaged in the most symbolic act of mothering – feeding her family. I add that the second time we see her, she is washing clothes with her arms, up to her elbows, in soapsuds, and the third time, she is trying to dress the cantankerous grandfather who is by now incapable of caring for his own basic needs. Occurring in quick succession on a busy morning, these are the housewife's most important tasks: feeding the family, keeping them clean, and tending to the needs of those too young or too old to do so for themselves. In these earliest scenes with Ma Joad, the family is making its final preparations for the journey to California, and women's work not only goes on almost uninterruptedly, but increases in intensity. The adults, though full of apprehensions, have high hopes that steady work and a return to stability await them at the end of the trip. They have seen handbills calling for laborers to come to California to reap the harvests of a rich and fruitful land. They believe the handbills, for who would go to the expense of printing misrepresentations of the situation?

Although at all times the Joads have very little or almost no money; and, while in Oklahoma, no realistic appraisal of how long the trip to California will take in their delapidated vehicle; and, in California, no assurances of how soon they will find work or a place to settle or know the nature of their future; an interesting aspect of Ma Joad's mothering psychology surfaces in different locations. On one hand, through most of the novel, she insists that her considerations are mainly for her family; on the other, she is willing to share the little food she has, to nurture whoever else is in need and comes along her way. We see this for the first time in Oklahoma, on first meeting her. Tom and his friend Casy arrive just as she completes the breakfast preparations on the day before the long, uncertain journey begins. Before she recognizes who they are, she invites them to partake of her board. Most notably, evidence of her largesse occurs again under more stressful circumstances, when she feeds a group of hungry children in California, although there is not sufficient food even for her family.

Another extension of Ma Joad's mothering precipitates her into a new and unaccustomed position of power within the family when she insists that Casy, with no family of his own, but who wishes to travel with them, be taken along. This is her first opportunity to assert herself outside of her housewife's role, to claim leadership in important decision making, whereas previously only the men officiated. Casy travels with the Joads only because Ma Joad overrides the objections of her husband, whose concerns for their space needs, and the small amount of money and little food they have, lead him to think it unwise to take an extra person, especially an outsider to the family, on the trip. Questioned on the matter, Ma replies:

> It ain't kin we? It's will we? . . . As far as 'kin,' we can't do nothin', not go to California or nothin'; but as far as 'will,' why, we'll do what we will. (139)

When the conversation ends, Casy has been accepted and she has gained new authority. She accepts this unpretentiously and with an absence of arrogance that will accompany her actions each time she finds it necessary to assert her will in the weeks and months ahead. And always, she asserts herself only for the good of the family. Two incidents that illustrate the group's understanding and acceptance of her wisdom and good judgment are especially noteworthy in this context. One occurs when the car breaks down during the journey and she refuses to agree to split up the family in order to hasten the arrival of some of its members in California. When her husband insists that separating is their better alternative, she openly defies him and, armed with a jack handle, challenges him to "whup" her first to gain her obedience to his will (230).[30] The second incident takes place in California, when, after weeks of the groups' unsuccessful search for work and a decent place to settle down, she chides the men for capitulating to despair. "You ain't got the right to get discouraged," she tells them, "this here fambly's goin' under. You jus' ain't got the right" (479).

But these situations, in which Ma's voice carries, also illustrate the tensions between men and women, in sex-gender-role systems, when women move into space traditionally designated to men. Each time Ma asserts her leadership she meets with Pa's resentment, for, regardless of her motives, he perceives that she usurps his authority. In the first instance, when Casy is accepted into the group, "Pa turned his back, and his spirit was raw from the whipping" her ascendancy represented to him (140). She, mindful of her role, leaves the family council and goes back to the house, to women's place, and women's work. But nothing takes place in her absence, the family waits for her return before continuing with their plans, "for she was powerful in the group" (140). During the trip (when Ma challenges Pa to "whup" her), after several suspenseful minutes, as the rest of the group watch his hands, the fists never form, and, in an effort to salvage his hurt pride, he can only say: "one person with their mind made up can shove a lot of folks aroun'!" (230). But again she is the victor and the "eyes of the whole family shifted back to Ma. She was the power. She had taken control" (231). Finally, in California, when Ma has her way once more in spite of Pa's opposition, and the family will move from a well-kept camp that had been a temporary respite from the traumas of the journey and their stay in Hooverville, but that placed them in an area in which they could find no work,

> Pa sniffled. "Seems like times is changed," he said sarcastically. "Time was when a man said what we'd do. Seems like women is tellin' now. Seems like it's purty near time to get out a stick." (481)

But he makes no attempt to beat her, for she quickly reminds him that men have the "right" to beat their women only when they (the men) are adequately performing their masculine roles.

"You get your stick Pa," she said. "Times when they's food an' a place to set, then maybe you can use your stick an' keep your skin whole. But you ain't a-doin' your job, either a-thinkin' or a-workin'. If you was, why, you could use your stick, an' women folks'd sniffle their nose an' creep-mouse aroun'. But you jus' get you a stick now an' you ain't lickin' no woman; you're a fightin', 'cause I got a stick all laid out too." (481)

In each of the instances mentioned here, once the decision is made and Ma's wise decision carries, she returns to women's place and/or displays stereotypical women's emotions. After her first confrontation with Pa over Casy, she hastens to tend the pot of "boiling side-meat and beet greens" to feed her family. Following the second, after she has challenged Pa to a fight and wins, she looks at the bar of iron and her hand trembles as she drops it on the ground. Finally, when she rouses the family from despair, she immediately resumes washing the breakfast dishes, "plunging" her hands into the bucket of water. And, to emphasize her selflessness, as her angry husband leaves the scene, she registers pride in her achievement, but not for herself. "He's all right," she notes to Tom. "He ain't beat. He's like as not to take a smack at me." Then she explains the aim of her "sassiness."

> Take a man, he can get worried an' worried, an' it eats out his liver, an' purty soon he'll jus' lay down and die with his heart et out. But if you can take an' make 'im mad, why, he'll be awright. Pa, he didn't say nothing', but he's mad now. He'll show me now. He's awright. (481)

Only once does Ma come face to face with the issue of gender roles, and the possibilities of recognizing women's oppression within the conventions of the patriarchal society, and that is in her early relationships with Casy, when, in her psychological embrace of him, he is no longer a stranger, or even a friend, he becomes one of the male members of the family. He thanks her for her decision to let him accompany them to California by offering to "salt down" the meat they will carry with them. To this offer, she is quick to point out that the task is "women's work" that need not concern him. It is interesting that the only crack in the ideology of a gender-based division of labor to occur in the novel is in Casy's reply to Ma, and his subsequent actions: "It's all work. . . . They's too much to do to split it up to men's and women's work. . . . Leave me salt the meat" (146). Although she permits him to do it, apparently, she learns nothing from the encounter, for it never becomes a part of her thinking. On the other hand, Casy's consciousness of the politics of class is in formation before we meet him in the novel and he is the only character in the book to realize that women are oppressed by the division of labor based on the differentiation of sex-gender roles.

If the wisdom that Steinbeck attributes to women directs Ma to step outside of her traditional role in times of crisis, as noted above, her actions immediately after also make it clear that she is just as willing to retreat to wifehood and motherdom. In this, she supports Steinbeck's championing of Briffault's theory that, in matriarchy, women do not seek to have authority over men. In her case, not even equality of place is sought, only the right to lead, for the good of the group, when her man is incapable of doing so. And Steinbeck suggests why women are better equipped to lead in time of great social stress: They are closer to nature and to the natural rhythms of the earth. When family morale is at its lowest point, Ma continues to nurture confidence: "Man, he lives in jerks – " she says, "baby born an' a man dies, an' that's a jerk – gets a farm an' loses his farm, an' that's a jerk." But women are different. They continue on in spite of the difficulties. "Woman, its all one flow, like a stream, little eddies, little waterfalls, but the river, it goes right on. Woman looks at it like that" (577). In times of crisis, Steinbeck suggests, the survival of the family and, by extension, the social order, depends on the wisdom and strength of the mother, whose interests are always those of her husband and children.

The long trek from Oklahoma to California provides many instances that demonstrate Ma's selfless nurturing, her wisdom, her leadership abilities, and, above all, her centeredness in the family. An important illustration of the latter occurs at the time of the death of the grandmother on the long night in which the family makes an incredibly precarious desert crossing into California. Lying with the dead old woman all night to conceal this partially unforeseen mishap from the rest of the group, Ma Joad's only thought during the ordeal is: "The fambly hadda get acrost" (312).

Alone with her secret of the true state of the old woman's condition, her considerations for the other members of the family, in this case particularly for the future of the younger children and for her daughter's unborn child, take precedence over the tremendous emotional cost to herself. Her determination to protect the family is almost ferocious, as she stands up to the officials at the agricultural inspection station on the California border to prevent them from discovering the dead woman by making a thorough check of the contents of the truck.

> Ma climbed heavily down from the truck. Her face was swollen and her eyes were hard. "Look, mister. We got a sick ol' lady. We got to get her to a doctor. We can't wait." She seemed to fight with hysteria. "You can't make us wait." (308)

Her apparent distress over the welfare of the old woman's health is convincing. One inspector perfunctorily waves the beam of his flashlight into the interior of the vehicle, and decides to let them pass. "I couldn' hold 'em" he tells his companion. "Maybe it was a bluff," the other replied, to which the first responded: "Oh, Jesus, no! You should of seen that ol' woman's face. That wasn't no bluff" (308). Ma is so intent on keeping the death a secret, even from the rest of the group as long as their overall situation remains threatening, that, when they arrive in the next town, she assures Tom that Granma is "awright – awright," and she implores him to "drive on. We got to get acrost" (308). She absorbs the trauma of the death in herself, and only after they have arrived safely on the other side of the desert does she give the information to the others. Even then she refuses the human touch that would unleash her own emotional vulnerability. The revelation of this act to protect the family is one of the most powerful scenes in the novel. The members of the family, already almost fully dependent on her emotional stamina, look at her "with a little terror at her strength" (312). Son Tom moves toward her in speechless admiration and attempts to put his hand on her shoulder to comfort her. "'Don' touch me,' she said. 'I'll hol' up if you don' touch me. That'd get me'" (312). And Casy, the newest member of the family, can only say: "there's a woman so great with love – she scares me" (313).

In Steinbeck's vision of a different and more humane society

than capitalistic greed spawned, he also believed that efforts like
Ma Joad's, to hold the family together in the way she always knew
it (individualism as a viable social dynamic), were doomed to
failure. Although she is unconscious of it at the time, her initial
embrace of Casy is a step toward a redefinition of family, and, by
the time the Joads arrive in California, other developments have
already changed the situation. Both Grampa and Granma are
dead. Soon after, son Noah, feeling himself a burden on the meager resources at hand, wanders away. In addition, Casy is mur-
dered for union activities; Al, whose mechanical genius was invaluable during the trip, is ready to marry and leave; Connie, Rose of
Sharon's husband, deserts, and her baby is stillborn; and Tom, in
an effort to avenge Casy's death, becomes a fugitive from the law
and decides to become a union organizer, to carry on Casy's work.
Through these events, first Tom, and then Ma, especially through
Tom's final conversation with her, achieve an education in the
politics of class oppression, and realize that the system that dimin-
ishes one family to the point of its physical and moral disintegration can only be destroyed through the cooperative efforts of those
of the oppressed group. "Use' ta be the fambly was fust. It ain't so
now. It's anybody," Ma is forced to admit toward the end of the
novel (606).

But, although the structure of the traditional family changes to
meet the needs of a changing society, in this novel at least, Steinbeck sees "happy-wife-and-motherdom" as the central role for
women, even for those with other significant contributions to
make to the world at large. Ma Joad's education in the possibilities
of class action do not extend to an awareness of women's lives and
identities beyond the domestic sphere, other than that which has a
direct relationship on the survival of the family. The conclusion of
the novel revises the boundaries of that family. In this scene, un-
able physically to supply milk from her own breasts to save the old
man's life, she initiates her daughter into the sisterhood of "mothering the world," of perpetuating what Nancy Chodorow calls
"The Reproduction of Mothering." Ma Joad is the epitome of the
Earth Mother. Critics note that Steinbeck need give her no first
name, for she is the paradigmatic mother, and this is the single
interest of her life. The seventeenth- and eighteenth-century meta-

phor of the fecund, virgin American land (women) gives way to
that of the middle-aged mother (earth), "thick with child-bearing
and work," but Steinbeck holds onto the stereotypical parallels
between woman and nature. In our typical understanding of that
word, Ma may not be happy in her role, but "her face . . . [is]
controlled and kindly" and she fully accepts her place. Having
"experienced all possible tragedy and . . . mounted pain and suffering like steps into a high calm," she fulfills her highest calling in
the realm of wife and motherdom.

## NOTES

1. I borrow from a phrase in Elizabeth Janeway's *Man's World, Woman's Place* (New York: William Morrow & Company, 1971), p. 151.
2. See Nancy Chodorow, *The Reproduction of Mothering: Psychoanalysis and the Sociology of Gender* (Berkeley: The University of California Press, 1978), p. 9.
3. Adrienne Rich, *Of Woman Born* (New York: W. W. Norton and Company, 1976).
4. See Note 1.
5. Nancy Chodorow, *The Reproduction of Motherhood: Psychoanalysis and the Sociology of Gender* (Berkeley: The University of California Press, 1978).
6. Hester Eisenstein, *Contemporary Feminist Thought* (Boston: G. K. Hall, 1983).
7. Eisenstein, p. 7. This is a point of view also expressed by almost all feminist critics.
8. Janeway, p. 13.
9. Ibid.
10. Chodorow, p. 9.
11. Janeway, pp. 192–208.
12. Chodorow, p. 179.
13. Annette Kolodny, *The Lay of the Land: Metaphor as Experience and History in American Life and Letters* (Chapel Hill: University of North California Press, 1975), p. 4.
14. Kolodny, pp. 5–9.
15. Ibid., p. 9.
16. John Steinbeck, *The Grapes of Wrath*, Peter Lisca, ed. (New York: Viking, 1972), p. 147. Subsequent references to this work are taken from this text.

17. See the scenes in which Ma Joad explains the conditions under which wives will allow themselves to be beaten without fighting back: pp. 230, 479.

18. Robert Briffault, *The Mothers: The Matriarchal Theory of Social Origins* (New York: Macmillan, 1931). Cited from Warren Motley, "From Patriarchy to Matriarchy: Ma Joad's Role in *The Grapes of Wrath, American Literature,* Vol. 54, No. 3, October 1982, pp. 397–411.

19. Mimi Reisel Gladstein, *The Indestructible Woman in Faulkner, Hemingway, and Steinbeck* (Ann Arbor, MI: University of Michigan Research Press, 1986), p. 79.

20. Peter Lisca, *The Wide World of John Steinbeck* (New Brunswick, NJ: Rutgers University Press, 1958), pp. 206–7. Quoted from Sandra Beatty, "A Study of Female Characterization in Steinbeck's Fiction," in Tetsumaro Hayashi, *Steinbeck's Women: Essays in Criticism* (Muncie, IN: The Steinbeck Society of America, 1979), p. 1.

21. Even though this is the prevailing opinion among critics of Steinbeck's women, I repeat it here to emphasize my basic agreement with this reading of the female characters. Steinbeck, like many male authors, sees a close link between woman as mother, nature, and the American land.

22. Gladstein, p. 76.

23. Sandra Falkenberg, "A Study of Female Characterization in Steinbeck's Fiction," in *Steinbeck Quarterly,* Vol. 8 (2), Spring 1975, pp. 50–6.

24. Howard Levant, "The Fully Matured Art: *The Grapes of Wrath,*" in *Modern Critical Views* edited and with an introduction by Harold Bloom (New York: Chelsea House Publishers, 1987), p. 35.

25. Joan Hedrick, "Mother Earth and Earth Mother: The Recasting of Myth in Steinbeck's *Grapes of Wrath,*" in The Grapes of Wrath: *A Collection of Critical Essays,* Robert Con Davis, ed. (Englewood Cliffs, NJ: G. K. Hall, 1982), p. 138.

26. Motley, p. 398.

27. Ibid., p. 405.

28. Chodorow, pp. 60–1.

29. See Kolodny, pp. 26–28 for an account of the high regard men like Thomas Jefferson had for the small farmer. In spite of the benefits of large-scale farming, he advocated the independent, family-size farm, and believed that those who tilled the earth gained "substantial and genuine virtue."

30. Ma Joad's challenge to her husband is that she be "whupped," not
    beaten. A woman may be beaten if her husband thinks she deserves
    it, and she accepts it without resistance. To be whipped indicates that
    she will fight back, and that he must win the fight in order to claim
    that he has whipped her.

# 4

# The Mother of Literature:
# Journalism and *The Grapes of Wrath*

### WILLIAM HOWARTH

What can I say about journalism? It has the greatest virtue and the greatest evil. It is the first thing the dictator controls. It is the mother of literature and the perpetrator of crap. In many cases it is the only history we have and yet it is the tool of the worst men. But over a long period of time and because it is the product of so many men, it is perhaps the purest thing we have. Honesty has a way of creeping in even when it was not intended.

> – John Steinbeck, letter to the U.S. Information Service (L526)

## The Rising Water

A T the end of *The Grapes of Wrath*, natural and human events impel the novel to a relentless climax. Far out at sea, early winter storms rise, sweep landward, and pour drenching rain on the California mountains. Streams cascade down into river valleys, flooding the lowlands where thousands of migrant families have set up makeshift camps. Many flee, others resist – and lose their meager goods to the rising water. Having no work or wages till spring, the migrants face a hopeless situation. They begin to starve, dying from exposure and disease, but no relief arrives. The Joad family faces an added crisis, as their daughter, Rose of Sharon, suffers through hard labor and delivers a stillborn child. Water forces the clan to higher ground, where they find a boy and his starving father. The young mother lies down beside the exhausted man. She bares her breast and he feeds.

Although perplexing to generations of readers, that final tableau fulfills a design that governs Steinbeck's entire novel.[1] His book opens with drought and ends with flood, waters that return to the earth and replenish its life. In saving a stranger, Rose of Sharon rises from brute survival instinct into a nurturing state of grace: "She looked up and across the barn, and her lips came together and smiled mysteriously" (619). His editor thought this ending was too enigmatic, but Steinbeck replied: "I've tried to make the reader participate in the actuality, what he takes from it will be scaled entirely on his own depth or hollowness. There are five layers in this book, a reader will find as many as he can and he won't find more than he has in himself" (L178–79).

In time readers have found plenty in *The Grapes of Wrath*, calling it a pack of lies, an American epic, an act of art wrapped in propaganda. This multeity of response bathed the author in ironies. His book denounced capitalism but rang up towering sales; its fame brought him wealth and power yet ruined him for greater work. "There is a failure here that topples all our success" (477), he wrote of the Depression, words that could also eulogize his own career. Why did this comet rise in his thirty-seventh summer, and what were its literary origins? Critics have tended to cite the modernist traditions of realism or symbolism, either aligning Steinbeck with social ideology – Farrell, Herbst, Wright – or with the cultural esthetics of Dos Passos and Faulkner.[2] Both traditions regard creativity as a lonely, heroic struggle, fought by artists for the sake of their people. Robert DeMott speaks for this consensus in calling *The Grapes of Wrath* "a private tragedy," in which the writer sacrificed "the unique qualities . . . that made his art exemplary" (W*xlvi*) to create a broad social novel.[3]

That vision of martyred demise may explain Steinbeck's later career, but it refutes the meaning of his greatest triumph. The novel's final scene is not a rite of sacrifice but fulfillment, as individual striving gives way to shared alliance. Two persons become one, not through sex or even love, but through their selfless flow into a broader stream, the rising water of human endurance. The novel repeats this idea in many contexts, most notably through Jim Casy, a prophet who fuses the socialist vision of class struggle with a sacramental longing for universal communion: "But when they're all workin' together, not one fella for another fella, but one fella kind of harnessed to the whole shebang – that's right, that's holy" (110). If these ideas hark back to Depression-era politics, they also anticipate a world that has yet to come, tied in bonds of ecological affinity.

Although Steinbeck praised collective action, he was no doctrinaire socialist, and critics have therefore placed him in a liberal ideology that regards the artist as both seer and entrepreneur: "The communal vision of *The Grapes of Wrath* began in the sweat of Steinbeck's lonely labor" (W*xxxii*), writes DeMott, whose edition of the novel's "work diary," with Jackson Benson's definitive biography, now give us a comprehensive view of the writer and his milieu. Their scholarship also reveals that Steinbeck's labors were far from lonely. Besides literature he drew constantly from the well of journalism, which he once called "the mother of literature" (L526). This debt was evident to Joseph Henry Jackson, who in 1940 first noted how *The Grapes of Wrath* borrowed its techniques from newsreel, photo-text, radio drama, and proletarian fiction – the peculiar hybrid forms of art, journalism, and propaganda that James Boylan calls *Depression reportage*. Reactions to that heritage fueled early quarrels over the book's literal accuracy and the New Critical emphasis on its mythology and philosophy. Another view is now in order, one suggesting that the mother of this novel – and its last maternal scene – was something Steinbeck knew as documentary.[4]

*Documentary* is a term used since the 1920s to denote the wedding of reportage, the investigative methods of journalism and sociology, to new forms of mass-media imagery, especially photography. Documentary is a didactic art that aims to look hard but feel soft, to affect an audience's emotions with ocular proof, the arrangement of apparently unselected scenes. The style tends to flourish in periods of grave social crisis, traumas that fracture public trust and arouse a clamor for indisputable facts. In this century the impulse has come in twenty- to thirty-year waves, from pre–World War I muckraking to the New Journalism of the Vietnam era. The Depression stands as a clear highwater mark, for during the 1930s there arose, in the words of historian William Stott, "a documentary imagination," determined to spread truth, right wrongs, and shape a new social order – one governed by the values of equity and cooperation. When Steinbeck alluded to the "five layers" in his book he was professing a documentary faith in data (he later said *Sea of Cortez* had four layers, L232), and in the emotional power of visual effects. Most important of these were his strong images, which emulated not the traditional arts of painting or sculpture but two popular forms of mass media, still and motion photography.[5]

The final chapters of *The Grapes of Wrath* exemplify this method by working through an intricate course of narrative "shots," from opening wide-angle panoramas of sea, air, and land to a tracking montage that follows the floodwaters' descent. This sequence of long- and mid-range images gathers into a fluent cascade of words:

> The rain beat on steadily. And the streams and the little rivers edged up to the bank sides and worked at willows and tree roots, bent the willows deep in the current, cut out the roots of cottonwoods and brought down the trees. The muddy water whirled along the bank sides and crept up the banks until at last it spilled over, into the fields, into the orchards, into the cotton patches where the black stems stood. Level fields became lakes, broad and gray, and the rain whipped up the surfaces. Then the water poured over the highways, and cars moved slowly, cutting the water ahead, and leaving a boiling muddy wake behind. The earth whispered under the beat of the rain, and the streams thundered under the churning freshets. (589–90)

At the river bottoms, these visual effects swiftly change from motion to contrast, an effect achieved by cross-cutting between the flood and the Joad family. Their faces appear in tight shots – portraits and extreme close-ups – that sharply differ from the epic anonymity of landscape and "the people." Such juxtapositions suggest equivalence, a strong parallelism between large and small events, the seen and unseen. As the Joad women struggle to deliver a child, their men labor to erect an earthen dike around a boxcar shelter. They succeed until a great cottonwood tree floats downstream, snags, and swings toward them:

> The water piled up behind. The tree moved and tore the bank. A little stream slipped through. Pa threw himself forward and jammed mud in the break. The water piled against the tree. And then the bank washed quickly down, washed around ankles, around knees.

Then men broke and ran, and the current worked smoothly into the flat, under the cars, under the automobiles.

Uncle John saw the water break through. In the murk he could see it. Uncontrollably his weight pulled him down. He went to his knees, and the tugging water swirled about his chest. . . .

When the dike swept out, Al turned and ran. His feet moved heavily. The water was about his calves when he reached the truck. He flung the tarpaulin off the nose and jumped into the car. He stepped on the starter. The engine turned over and over, and there was no bark of the motor. He choked the engine deeply. The battery turned the sodden motor more and more slowly, and there was no cough. Over and over, slower and slower. (601–2)

The visible events — snagged tree, breached dike, dead engine — intimate an unseen drama transpiring in the boxcar, as Rose of Sharon labors through her stillbirth. Narration is thus working in two focal planes, exterior foreshadowing interior, with Steinbeck shifting from natural panorama to human close-up, one cause to another effect:

The air was fetid and close with the smell of the birth. Uncle John clambered in and held himself upright against the side of the car. Mrs. Wainwright left her work and came to Pa. She pulled him by the elbow toward the corner of the car. She picked up a lantern and held it over an apple box in the corner. On a newspaper lay a blue shriveled little mummy.

"Never breathed," said Mrs. Wainwright softly. "Never was alive."

Uncle John turned and shuffled tiredly down the car to the dark end. The rain whished softly on the roof now, so softly that they could hear Uncle John's tired sniffling from the dark. (603)

Rainfall merges with tears, just as the floodwaters will give way to a mother's milk. Throughout the novel Steinbeck oscillates from large- to small-scale events, building a dialectic between nature and humanity, the masses and the Joad family. This synecdochal linkage is an ancient narrative device, common to folk and scriptural sagas, that gives *The Grapes of Wrath* its epic dimensions. The principle is also visual, moving from distance to foreground and back again to provide pictorial scale and depth. Steinbeck was quite aware of this formal method, alluding frequently in his work diary to a plan of alternating "general" and "particular" chapters

(W23, 39).[6] That plan arose from a simple paradox: His book really began with its ending.

## On Assignment

The final chapters of *The Grapes of Wrath* represent actual events that Steinbeck witnessed in February, 1938, near Visalia, California. Unusually prolonged rain that winter produced high floods along the local streams, stranding over 5,000 migrant families in homeless destitution. For several days Steinbeck joined relief efforts there, moving families and caring for the sick. People were dying from cholera or starvation, often simply dropping dead in their tracks. He later said the experience hurt inside, "clear to the back of my head" (W*xliii*), and the probable source of pain was guilt. After passing some years as a raffish bohemian he had attained the status of best-selling author, enriched by stage and film adaptations of his books. His sympathy for victims of the Depression was clear, but so, too, was the fact that he earned a living as chronicler of their pain: "Funny how mean and little books become in the face of such tragedies" (L159).[7]

In fact, his purpose at Visalia was twofold: to garner publicity for federal efforts at flood relief, and to gather material for a text-and-picture book about California's farm migrants. The latter project was proposed to him in late 1937 by Horace Bristol, a San Francisco photographer with many story credits at *Life*. For several weekends they had traveled throughout the Central Valley, operating as a team to capture interviews and images. Steinbeck was a natural collaborator, Bristol recalled: "He'd get to talking to somebody, and I'd move in behind him with the camera." Using a twin-lens reflex in natural light, Bristol took unposed, candid shots of people at close- or midrange – wading in knee-deep water, standing before tent homes and mired autos. One picture, of a young mother nursing her baby, was later widely assumed to be the model of Rose of Sharon. In all, he exposed over 2,000 frames, and in the process he strongly affected Steinbeck's vision of the migrants. In early March the writer told his literary agent "we took a lot of pictures," adding that the images "give you an idea of the kind of people they are and the kind of faces" (L161).[8]

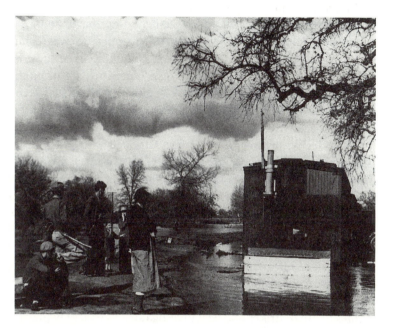

Horace Bristol: Flooded boxcar home near Visalia, 1938. Courtesy of Horace Bristol.

After the Visalia experience, Steinbeck brooded on how best to write about those people. Bristol envisioned a book like *You Have Seen Their Faces* (1938), an album on Southern sharecroppers by Erskine Caldwell and Margaret Bourke-White. To publicize this goal, Bristol negotiated with editors at Time, Inc. for a major photo-essay. Steinbeck rejected a lucrative deal with *Fortune* as inappropriate, but he agreed to an offer from *Life* that covered expenses and a donation to flood relief (L162). The team submitted a story, which *Life* chose not to publish at that time. Defiantly, Steinbeck placed a strong news report, called "Starvation under the Orange Trees," in the *Monterey Trader* (April 15, 1938). By late spring Bristol had selected his pictures for the book, only to find that Steinbeck had other plans: "Well, Horace, I'm sorry to tell you, but I've decided it's too big a story to be just a photographic book. I'm going to write it as a novel."[9]

In a 1951 reminiscence, Steinbeck wrote of his father: "To be anything pure requires an arrogance he did not have, and a selfishness he could not bring himself to assume. He was a man intensely disappointed in himself. And I think he liked the complete ruthlessness of my design to be a writer in spite of mother and hell" (W140). Back in mid-1938 Horace Bristol had seen a flash of the writer's arrogance and its ruthless designs. From then on Steinbeck rarely acknowledged working with Bristol or the effect of seeing his migrant pictures. Although Bristol lost or destroyed most of the photographs, he published a surviving handful in 1989. By then he was inclined to forgive, if not forget, Steinbeck's slight: "He was secretive, and he wanted to feel that anything he did was his, and nobody else had any influence on it."[10]

In spurning Bristol, Steinbeck also concealed the fact that since 1936 he had pursued "The Matter of Migrants," as he called plans for a book of his own. He kept this work secret mainly because it was controversial and dangerous. Labor strife pitted the government against California's Associated Farmers, who often hired vigilantes to break strikes and beat investigators. Fearful of betrayal or retaliation, Steinbeck worked undercover and incognito. Using journalistic assignments to underwrite his field trips, he took data wherever he found it – readings, interviews, background briefings – and borrowed stories freely, in the name of public interest. Given these methods, he had trouble deciding whether his book should be factual or fictional, and what his stake was in its creation.[11] Sometimes the goal was selfless advocacy, rather than popularity: "I want this book to be itself with no history and no writer" (L181). At other times ambition led him on, toward the alluring goal of fame. An echo of that conflict resounds in his novel: Before leaving Oklahoma, Ma Joad burns her precious box of "letters, clippings, photographs" and keeps a few bits of gold jewelry (148).

### The Writer as Reporter

This wayward journey began when Steinbeck published "Dubious Battle in California," a brief essay about labor migrants in *The Nation* (September 13, 1936), and then agreed to write a series of investigative articles for the *San Francisco News*. He obtained major assistance from Farm Security Administration (FSA) documents, including reports compiled by Tom Collins, manager of a federal camp for migrants at Arvin. Collins, a psychologist with a flair for writing, had extensively interviewed his residents and gathered a thick compendium of their stories, songs, and folklore, interpolated with his own descriptions and impressions. He generously lent this material to Steinbeck, who used it and his own notes (gathered on trips with Collins) to write "The Harvest Gypsies," a seven-part series for the *News* (Oct. 5–11, 1936). The project won widespread attention, in part for Steinbeck's impassioned, detailed reporting and in part for several pictures shot by Dorothea Lange, an acclaimed FSA photographer.[12]

Steinbeck's association with the FSA gave him contact with a federal agency that effectively used documentary photos to promote New Deal programs. Guided by Roy Stryker, the Historical Section of the FSA compiled over 270,000 images of American life in 1935–43, much of it shot by such leading photographers as Lange, Walker Evans, Russell Lee, Arthur Rothstein, Gordon Parks, and Ben Shahn. Stryker set high technical standards for their pictures, calling for an emphasis on individual portraits rather than mobs of striking field hands. The results were often idealized pictures of decent, dignified folk who were blamelessly down on their luck. Dorothea Lange specialized in what William Stott aptly calls "the worthy poor," people of low status whose portraits maintained a quality of intimacy and poignancy for their middle-class viewers. Her style of work embraced the inherent tenets of documentary, authenticity heightened by emotional appeal. With resolute control she chose her subjects, posed them carefully, and supervised the processing of negatives and prints. At the same time she was candid about this work and its purposes, unlike the shy, secretive Steinbeck.[13]

The migrant stories won wide attention in the *News* and even more when reprinted as a pamphlet, *Their Blood Is Strong* (1938), by the prolabor Simon J. Lubin Society. On the cover was Lange's photo of a young woman in a tent shelter, nursing her child. The final scene of *The Grapes of Wrath* may have borrowed from this image, which projects a striking aura of ambiguity. Seated in a makeshift cluttered space, the woman looks straight ahead with a calm, impassive expression. Her face and body are youthful, having the strong planes and curves that a lens favors, but her bared breast leads the eye to the central figure, a child's wide-eyed, demanding face. Other shots of this scene include a man in the foreground; in this picture, his legs are partially visible. Linked to Steinbeck's title phrase, the cover shot was designed to stir feelings of racial pride, for his text made clear that the migrants' strong blood flowed in Anglo-Saxon veins. Yet the image also illustrates the ambivalence of documentary: Years later, William Stott saw a woman with "the innocent trapped eyes of a deer" while feminist Wendy Kozol saw one "assertive in her direct gaze." Both viewers recognized one of the FSA's stereotypical genres, the nurturing Madonna, who appealed strongly to middle-class readers.[14]

Throughout 1937 Steinbeck cast about for his book on the migrants, wavering between the poles of fact and fiction. Impressed with the "great gobs of information" (W*lii*) in Tom Collins's camp reports, he offered to help edit them into a diarylike narrative that "would make one of the greatest and most authentic and hopeful human documents I know" (B348). At the same time, Steinbeck envisioned writing an epic novel, tentatively called "The Oklahomans," about the migrants' journey to California (W*xxxvii*). To advance both plans, he and Collins made extensive Central Valley trips in the summer and fall of 1937, visiting squatters' camps and working as field hands. These experiences confirmed the accuracy of Collins's reports, which Steinbeck saw as a source to keep the novel honest, safe from charges of lying (W*xxviii*). Yet by winter both projects subsided and Steinbeck instead accepted Horace Bristol's proposal to collaborate on a picture book. They began to travel on weekends, sometimes accompanied by Collins.

When the floods hit Visalia in February 1938, Steinbeck again found himself caught between literary and journalistic impulses. Frustrated by poor coverage in local newspapers, officials at the FSA asked him to write some reports for national circulation. He saw this task as a humanitarian mission: "I'm going to try to break the story hard enough so that food and drugs can get moving. . . . If I can sell the articles I'll use the proceeds for serum and such" (L159). During this time negotiations went forward with *Fortune*

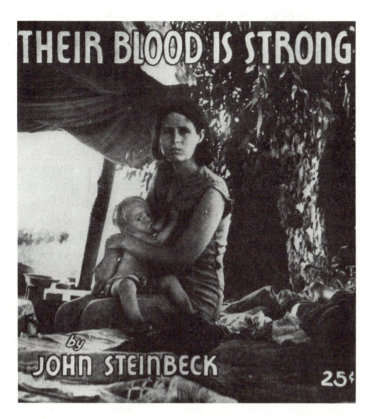

Dorothea Lange: Partial front cover of *Their Blood Is Strong*. Courtesy of Steinbeck Research Center.

and *Life*, and by March he had filed the story. Yet, by choosing *Life* to publicize the migrants, Steinbeck had thrown in his lot with a photographer's magazine, not a writer's. The pages of *Life* featured huge images, printed with such clarity and depth of focus that they created the illusion of complete authenticity. The result was strong propaganda, echoing formulas followed by *Der Spiegel* and *Stern* in Nazi Germany.

No less strident was Steinbeck's concurrent effort to write a novel, called "L'Affaire Lettuceberg," about a farm labor strike.

Intended as satire, the project soon degenerated into a bitter tract, its sarcasm sharply contrasting with the generous spirit of his Visalia story. By May he completed a draft but then declined to publish it, telling his agent that the work was too biased and incomplete: "Oh! these incidents all happened but – I'm not telling as much of the truth about them as I know. . . . My whole work drive has been aimed at making people understand each other and then I deliberately write this book the aim of which is to cause hatred through partial understanding. . . . A book must be a life that lives all of itself and this one doesn't do that" (W*xl*).

A book "that lives all of itself" would merge advocacy with altruism, and this documentary standard had arisen since Steinbeck's experiences in Visalia. The flood scenes and pictures began to focus his previous attempts to write about migrants. To date, the Collins reports and his own drafts had yielded three different stories: life in the camps, the journey west, and strikes. In the Visalia experience Steinbeck now saw a climactic episode that fused those materials. A five-part narrative sequence – drought, flight, camp, strike, and flood – would encompass the migrants' entire history and geography. His story plan thus emerged: alternating chapters, strong visual images, themes of sharing versus greed. Steinbeck's two-year search was over, and in that moment of triumph he cast aside his collaborators.

Tom Collins proved least disposable, for his camp reports were so invaluable that Steinbeck dedicated the novel "To TOM who lived it" and used him as a model for Jim Rawley, manager of the Weedpatch camp. But Horace Bristol had to go, not because his photographs were inappropriate, but too influential. The claim that Visalia was "too big a story to be just a photographic book" belied the fact that pictures helped Steinbeck find a narrative plan and stylistic model. And if the story was too big for photos, why did it have to be fiction? He had aborted four previous efforts, two novels and two documentaries, in which the elements of actuality and imagination would not coalesce. The migrant story begged for documentation, since many facts were in dispute, but most critics believe that somehow Steinbeck lost his reportorial appetite at Visalia. Joseph Millichap writes, "The reality he encountered seemed too significant for nonfiction," an opinion echoed by

Robert DeMott: ". . . he was utterly transfixed by the 'staggering' condition, and by 'suffering' so great that objective reporting would only falsify the moment" (W*xlii*).[15]

Steinbeck refutes that notion of reportage in the very letter cited, attacking "slick" magazines like *Fortune* and *Life*, but not all periodical journalism: "I want to put a tag of shame on the greedy bastards who are responsible for [neglecting the migrants] but I can do it best through newspapers" (L162). Even so, his energy soon shifted to creating the Joad family, a fictional cast that DeMott says "elevated the entire history of the migrant struggle into the ceremonial realm of art" (W*xliii*). This sacramental view corresponds to a general belief that the Joads are mythical questers, but considerable evidence also points to their origin in documentary sources. From Collins, Lange, and Bristol, Steinbeck gleaned several text-and-picture portraits that suggested his family characters. *Life* later confirmed that parallel, by printing Bristol's pictures with captions from *The Grapes of Wrath*.[16]

The notion that Steinbeck turned to fiction because it was a higher, truer form of expression betrays either his intellect or his documentary principles. He chose fiction to make his story more artful, not truthful. In fiction he could fabricate at will, making up people and events by splicing and reshaping materials gathered from research. The decision to anchor his "particular" story in a family of characters was inspired but hardly original, for many documentaries did the same in order to dramatize social history. The Joads were both individual and universal; they gave the story credibility rather than authenticity. As Mark Twain once remarked, "Truth is stranger than Fiction . . . because Fiction is obliged to stick to possibilities. Truth isn't." Yet *The Grapes of Wrath* is often truthful because it strives to emulate documentary genres: case study, informant narrative, travel report, photo-text. Steinbeck wanted his migrant book to be honest and moral, an act of social expiation. As he wrote his agent, "I'm trying to write history while it is happening and I don't want to be wrong" (L162). Instead, the book reaped great profit and notoriety, both further obscuring its documentary origins. That source was clearer in June, 1938, as he began the manuscript headed "New Start/Big Writing" and also a daily log.[17]

## Diary and Novel

Of all his working papers – news clips, government briefs, reports, and letters – none were more valuable to Steinbeck than the private journal, or "daily work diary" (W39), that he kept during the five-month process of writing *The Grapes of Wrath*. The diary served several functions, practical and psychological, but it was always more than just a craftsman's tool. Steinbeck attached a totemic significance to his writing habits, from a pen and ruled notebook to his small room and enforced hours of quiet labor. The diary was his gateway to and from his work, allowing him to pass into the narrative and back out to daily life. Writing an entry each morning replaced his usual letters but maintained their aspect of dialogue: "Must make note of work progress at the end of this day. I want to finish my stint if I possibly can. Impulses to do other things. Wind blowing over me, etc." (W21).

He was talking to and of himself, in that subject–object blurring that invokes character, and some of his mood probably emanated from a scene just completed in Chapter 4, where Tom Joad and Jim Casy discuss the conflict between duty and impulse, body and spirit: "Maybe all men got one big soul ever'body's a part of," Casy concludes (33). That was true in the unitary realm of imagination, but in the diary Steinbeck also recorded his schisms, moments when all the world's distractions – friends, talk, drink, sex, money, news – sundered his concentration, broke his confidence in the story. The diary offered a disciplinary ritual, each day launching, sustaining, and focusing his efforts, admitting him to a realm where reality and fiction were coeval: "In ten days I will be half done. 50 days of work. I hope we get to California by then because I would like half the time out here" (W46). The "I" and "we" referred to himself and his characters or, alternately, to writer and diary. In the isolation of his work, its pages became his final collaborator.

Besides documenting his progress the diary shaped its direction, turning his writing into a journey that paralleled the Joads'. Much of the plot outline arose from his decision to begin in Oklahoma, for that impelled the story to move constantly forward, each chapter rolling west along "the main migrant road" to reach California

(160). The "unity feeling" (W27) Steinbeck often sensed while writing arose from identifying his own motion, line by line and page by page, with the miles slipping past his characters. He calculated time and distance in words, not cash or fuel, striving "to try to maintain a certain writing speed" (W25). At times writing was like Tom Joad's prison term, "Must not think too much of the end but of the immediate story – instant and immediate" (W38), for, in each given moment of composition, the story had a fluid momentum of its own: "And so the book moves on steadily, forcefully, slowly, and it must continue to move slowly. How I love it" (W31).

This sense of inevitability encouraged him to emulate the characters at many levels, sharing their losses, determined to survive by going on: "Can't tell. Can't tell. Just have to plod for 90,000 words. Plod as the people are plodding. They aren't rushing" (W59). His dogged fatalism advanced him in a fairly straight line, with fewer stalls and breakdowns than the migrants, though at times he puzzled over how plot sequences "mapped out" (W72) or he turned from linear progress to make adjustments: "Must go back and send Noah down the river" (W73). And so the writing went, fast or slow, mirroring the Joads' progress and enhancing their story with the mythic aura of westering, the American journey sustained by an indomitable work ethic: "I'll get the book done if I just set one day's work in front of the last day's work. That's the way it comes out. And that's the only way it does" (W85). He was then writing Chapter 26, where the martyred Jim Casy asserts that human progress is inevitable (525), echoing Ma Joad's earlier sentiment, "Why, we're the people – we go on" (383).

The diary was not fiction, but a fact book; it monitored his progress, corrected errors, curbed the impulse to stray from sources. He sensed quite early that this arbiter would hold him to documentary standards: "I have tried to keep diaries before but they don't work out because of the necessity to be honest. In matters where there is no definite truth, I gravitate toward the opposite" (W19). But this diary linked those opposites, allowing him to enter and exit the story, to write alternating units – "Yesterday the general and now back to the particular" (W23) – and to rein in his imagination: "The more I think of it, the better I like this work diary idea. Always I've set things down to loosen up a creaking mind but never have I done so consecutively. This sort of keeps it all corralled in one place" (W42). Discipline yielded force, but not always conscious control. "I did it but it may not be good. I don't know. But it is in, the I to We" (W43). He had just finished Chapter 14, on the growth of revolutionary masses, and the same transfer of power was beginning to affect his book: "For the quality of owning freezes you forever into 'I,' and cuts you off forever from the 'we' " (206).

If Steinbeck did not live by that ideal (he was then buying a new ranch, the biggest property deal of his life – W15),[18] he at least wrote toward it, for the diary and book had acquired an autonomy, in which he participated as both inventor and recorder: "Often in writing these beginning lines I think it is going to be all right and then it isn't. Just have to see. I hope it is all right today" (W46). Although his life was especially fractious at this time, his work had an energetic spontaneity of its own: "Where has my discipline gone? Have I lost control? Quite coldly we'll see today. See whether life comes into the lives and the people move and talk. We'll see. Got her, by God" (W61). Somewhere between seeing and shaping lay the story. He could push characters about and make events happen, but also just open himself to intuitive possibilities: "Got to get them out of Hooverville and into a federal camp for they must learn something of democratic procedure. . . . The flow of story is coming back to me. The feel of the people. And the feel of speech and the flow of action. So it must go and if it takes until Christmas, then that is the way it must be" (W64–5).

As the story reached its late stages, narrative momentum became a compelling force. His daily exhortations took on a quality of passionate testimony: "This is the important part of the book. Must get it down. This little strike. Must win it. Must be full of movement, and it must have the fierceness of the strike. And it must be won" (W79). Of course the story was not writing itself, but increasingly he cast himself as its witness or reporter, just giving an account of what passed before his eyes: "And my story is coming better. I see it better. See it better. . . . Half an hour gone already and I don't care because the little details are coming, are getting clearer all the time" (W82–3).

### Pictures Still and Moving

The work diary often reveals how persistently Steinbeck described his imagination in photographic terms, as though his mental images arose from an unmediated source. Like pictures in a tray of developer, the final scenes emerged slowly but with startling clarity. He had known from the outset how and where the story would end, but getting there proved difficult, for he had incorrectly calculated the term of Rose of Sharon's pregnancy (W72). If she were to deliver at full term in winter, that would mean conception back in the spring, before the novel begins. He fixed this by having Pa vaguely announce, "An' Rosasharn's due 'bout three–four–five months now" (113) and later describing the stillborn infant as premature, "a blue shriveled little mummy" (603). Nervous doubts arose about the flood and birth sequence (W86), but he resolved them by letting his plan emerge from the characters' needs: "The last general must be a summing of the whole thing. Group survival. Yes, I am excited. Almost prayerful that this book is some good. Maybe it is and maybe not. Now let's see what we have" (W88).

That "we" was a group that survived through labor and love, for in coming to closure Steinbeck felt a mixture of "plain terror" and "some kind of release" at his prospect of loss (W92). To pass this barrier he reread the work diary, seeing in its pages a visual image of his creative process: "And I think I have every single move mapped out for the ending. I only hope it is good. It simply has to be. Well, there it is, all of it in my mind" (W92). This mental habit may reflect the continuing effect of Horace Bristol's pictures, later recognized by *Life* as a principal source for *The Grapes of Wrath:* "Never before had the facts behind a great work of fiction been so carefully researched by the newscamera." Robert DeMott insists that the writer and camera saw events quite differently, right up to the final scene. He argues that Bristol's picture is merely of a mother nursing an infant, while Rose of Sharon gives her breast to a starving man, "a leap beyond facticity" (W*lvi*).

That term forces a distinction, since the usual signifiers (*factitious* and *fictitious*) both mean contrived, made artificially. Like all photographs, Bristol's picture is not reality but its representation, flattened to the constraints of two dimensions and one moment. As Susan Sontag notes, photographs are artifacts that also seem "to have the status of found objects – unpremeditated slices of the world." Bristol's image of the nursing mother may appear to be self-evident, yet its formal aspects – angle, elevation, focus, depth, frame, light, and shadow – all reflect his work as a selective, shaping recorder.[19] In substituting a man for a baby, Steinbeck slipped into double exposure, superimposing memories of other photos (Lange's no doubt included) on scenes he witnessed at Visalia: "[I]n our agricultural valleys, I've seen a family that was hungry give all its food to a family that was starving. I suppose that is inspiration. It and things like it only make me feel like a rat" (W142). Such images of instinctive generosity compelled him to foresee the entire book, including "the last scene, huge and symbolic, toward which the whole story moves," as a humbling revelation: "I felt very small and inadequate and incapable but I grew again to love the story which is so much greater than I am" (W36).

This attitude led him to see the book in iconic terms, consistent with the values of modern photojournalism. The persistent focus on cars and highways matched FSA standards,[20] as did the alternation of near and far views: "This is a huge job. Mustn't think of its largeness but only of the little picture while I am working. Leave the large picture for planning time" (W29). To him the characters were figures who moved in and out of focus: "Watch the old people. Might get out of hand but I want them mean and funny" (W30), and in those two dimensions they shifted constantly between his needs and theirs: "Make the people live. Make them live. But my people must be more than people. They must be an over-essence of people" (W39). They should be *and* mean, existing apart but also within him. Hence their departures aroused his fierce empathy – the death of Grampa Joad made Steinbeck write ". . . once this book is done I won't care how soon I die" (W41), while Tom Joad's farewell induced an apparent hallucination: "I hope the close isn't controlled by my weariness. . . . 'Tom! Tom! Tom!' I know. It wasn't him. Yes, I think I can go on now. In fact, I feel stronger. Much stronger. Funny where the energy comes from" (W91).

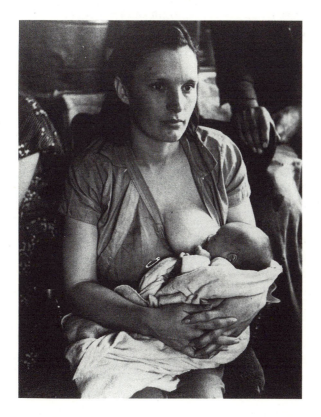

Horace Bristol: Young mother and newborn, Visalia, 1938.
Courtesy of Horace Bristol.

The energy of *The Grapes of Wrath* came not just from still photography but also from motion pictures, a source that Steinbeck more openly acknowledged as influential. Principles of cinematic narrative sprang directly from fiction, and by 1938 Steinbeck had absorbed enough movies to recognize their enormous power to move and inform. Most of his 1930s novels have strong filmic qualities, which accounts for their swift adaptation into screenplays, work that he assisted by suggesting locations and reading draft treatments. Film rights to *Of Mice and Men* sold easily, but in the early stages of writing *The Grapes of Wrath* he waved off an inquiry from the Selznick company as premature, telling his agent "no picture company would want this new book whole" because it was too controversial (L168). Hollywood in the 1930s did offer him many liberal friends, including the actors Wallace Ford, Broderick Crawford, and Charlie Chaplin. But the most influential film maker of all was Pare Lorentz, the brilliant documentarian whom Steinbeck first met in January 1938, just prior to going to Visalia.[21]

Lorentz was anything but Hollywood, for he created highly original films (and radio plays) about such unpromising subjects as soil conservation and flood control. As head of the U. S. Film Service from 1935 to 1940, he worked on low budgets but managed to orchestrate the talents of top writers, photographers, and directors. Two of his films, *The Plow That Broke the Plains* (1936) and *The River* (1937) established new standards in American documentary, bringing lyricism and epic scale to the promotion of New Deal programs. Lorentz made his films encompass vast sweeps of history, from the settlement of the prairies to the Depression crisis, and he was able to dramatize vividly how economic and social forces had shaped the American land and people. *The River* was his tour de force, employing imagery and sound in complex patterns to describe the Mississippi Basin and its ecological fate. Especially effective was Lorentz's incantatory text, simple phrasings intoned by Thomas Chalmers, a Met baritone, to accompany a fluid montage of images and music scored by Virgil Thompson.[22]

Lorentz and his films were on Steinbeck's mind throughout early 1938, as he groped with his various writings on migrants. Lorentz helped midwife *The Grapes of Wrath* by placing "Starvation under the Orange Trees" in the Monterey paper, and then dissuading Steinbeck from further work on his strike novel, "L'Affaire Lettuceberg" (B371–2, W151). The two men also talked of film collaboration, either by adapting a Steinbeck novel such as *In Dubious Battle,* or by producing an original screenplay. Yet as Steinbeck pursued his "Big Writing" he developed characteristic hesitations. In August, Lorentz read early chapters and praised them highly, which encouraged the writer to press on – and, as he wrote in the diary, to stay clear of films: "I do hope that Pare won't need me, much as I'd like to work with him. I must do my own work and I have a feeling that he is this picture not me" (W65).

90

Just as he had withdrawn from Collins and Bristol, Steinbeck evaded Lorentz while absorbing the effect of his style and ideas. One of Lorentz's radio dramas closed with a stirring rendition of "The Battle Hymn of the Republic," which may have suggested *The Grapes of Wrath* as a title to Steinbeck's wife, Carol (W*xxvi*). The grateful author later rewarded her with a dedication, "To CAROL who willed this book," for on one level he regarded his novel as autogenous, self-created, and sustaining: "The looks of it – that marvelous title. The book has being at last" (W65). His fiction also emulated Lorentz's narrative principles, shifting from foreground to background, cutting from panorama to close-up, providing choric and lyric commentary in the expository chapters. Steinbeck later acknowledged that his most conspicuous borrowing was for Chapter 12, the naming of towns along Route 66: "I have little doubt that the Lorentz River is strong in that" (W*li*).

The work diary reflects other parallels, for he frequently described the novel in cinematic terms, as pictures or scenes that move: ". . . the movement is so fascinating that I don't stay tired. . . . slow but sure, piling detail on detail until a picture and an experience emerge. Until the whole throbbing thing emerges" (W25). He played this action out in settings, the physical locations – porch, road, gas station – that gave strong scenic values to his themes. Chapter 15 begins in what Steinbeck called "an important place" (W44), a hamburger stand that he describes entirely in sentence fragments. Action and continuity in the sequence come from visual tracking rather than verbs:

> At one end of the counter a covered case; candy cough drops, caffeine sulphate called Sleepless, No-Doze; candy, cigarettes, razor blades, aspirin, Bromo-Seltzer, Alka-Seltzer. The walls decorated with posters, bathing girls, blondes with big breasts and slender hips and waxen faces, in white bathing suits, and holding a bottle of Coca-Cola and smiling – see what you get with a Coca-Cola. Long bar, and salts, peppers, mustard pots, and paper napkins. Beer taps behind the counter, and in back the coffee urns, shiny and steaming, with glass gauges showing the coffee level. And pies in wire cages and oranges in pyramids of four. And little piles of Post Toasties, corn flakes, stacked up in designs. (208)

The passage illustrates why Steinbeck chose to write fiction rather than documentary, for despite all its concrete detail this place is imaginary, a broad, generic description that is "typical" instead of literal.[23] Suppression of the verbs also disrupts normal syntactic relations between subject and object, so that the scene plays not through a narrator or character, but through a transparent viewer. The result is prose that emulates film, less from the perspective of a director or editor than of a sensitive observer, which at the time is mainly how Steinbeck knew movies.

In writing *The Grapes of Wrath* he drew closer to film techniques, even while dodging requests to write screenplays for Lorentz or actor Paul Muni, who wanted to adapt *Tortilla Flat* (W76). The later chapters became especially cinematic in style, as they picked up the writer's sense of driving momentum: "Just a little bit every day. A little bit every day. And then it will be through. And the story is coming to me fast now. And it will be fast from now on. Movement fast but the detail slow as always" (W83). While he had brief doubts about including the flood (W86), he resolved them by creating a sequence that imitates the opening and middle parts of *The River,* where water rises high in the mountains and tumbles down to drowned valleys (589ff). Letters from Lorentz arrived as Steinbeck wrote this section, rousing thoughts of a film and doubts about his novel: "The rain – the birth – the flood –and the barn. The starving man and the last scene that has been ready so long. I don't know. I only hope it is some good. I have very grave doubts sometimes. . . . I am sure of one thing – it isn't the great book I had hoped it would be. It's just a run-of-the-mill book. And the awful thing is that it is absolutely the best I can do" (W88–90).

Some of this despairing mood came from exhaustion and a performer's lack of perspective, but Steinbeck also sensed a disparity between his story and talent. In February the floods at Visalia had filled him with anguish; now, in mid-October, they threatened once more. With so much material at hand, sources compiled and edited into a new order, he carried a lonely burden: "Well, I might as well get to the work. No one is going to do it for me" (W92). Yet, in mounting the drive toward completion, he saw himself mainly as a reporter: "Forget that it is the finish and just set down the day by day work. . . . Best way is just to get down to the lines. . . . Finished this day – and I hope to God it's good" (W92–3). This ambivalence about his role may account for a later remark, that he wrote *The Grapes of Wrath* "in a musical technique" governed by mathematical principles, for such abstractions would also limit his authorial responsibility (W13).

## Aftermath

In the months that followed completion of his "Big Writing," Steinbeck turned with relief back to collective ventures. Filming of *The Grapes of Wrath* in late 1939 involved him in a reprise of the novel's creation: Tom Collins worked as a technical advisor, while director John Ford consulted Lange's photos and Lorentz's films for stylistic pointers. Even Horace Bristol finally got some attention, for *Life* published his photos to verify the accuracy of both novel and film. As Joseph Millichap confirms, Ford's film imitates the look of documentary rather than its feel, softening Steinbeck's political themes by emphasizing nostalgia over anger, the Joads over the masses, and eliminating entirely the novel's general chapters.[24] Yet, after its opening in January, 1940, it was an enormously popular film and undoubtedly helped to prolong the novel's public recognition.

The firestorm of protest that greeted *The Grapes of Wrath*, most of it raging over the book's "truth," ultimately eroded its efficacy as a social document. Public interest in rural poverty waxed and soon waned, creating little market for such documentary treatments as Carey McWilliams's *Factories in the Field* (1939), Dorothea Lange and Paul Taylor's *An American Exodus* (1939), or James Agee and Walker Evans's *Let Us Now Praise Famous Men* (1941).[25] Yet celebrity gave Steinbeck himself many opportunities to pursue documentary projects. He did finally collaborate with Lorentz on *The Fight for Life* (1939), a screenplay about infant mortality, and then wrote both story and script for *The Forgotten Village* (1941), on the coming of modern medicine to rural Mexico. In his preface to the film's published text Steinbeck justified his use of fictional devices, such as telling the story through one family, asking villagers to re-enact events, and providing choric commentary through an offscreen narrator, "so natural and unobtrusive that an audience would not even be conscious of it."[26]

After that came *Sea of Cortez* (1941), an account of a marine biological expedition that Steinbeck edited from trip logs, adding considerable form and poetry of his own, according to "coauthor" Ed Ricketts (W104–5). And then World War Two swept in, years when tumult compelled the writer back into a welcome role of social duty, where he wrote training films and dispatches for a cause that had few detractors. His remaining years were to be crowded and productive, often with projects that featured reporting and photography. But never again did he reach the highwater mark of *The Grapes of Wrath*, a book that began in flood and ended with a vision of the enduring human family.

In moving toward that close, the novel passes through its alternating phases of wind and water, fruition and decay, junked cars and the relentless "fury of work" (599) that drives people forward, ever determined to survive despite the constancy of gain and loss. Beginning in the center of America, the migrants find at the continent's edge that Eden still lies elsewhere, down the road that pulls them with the relentless tug of a future. While alternating chapters give *The Grapes of Wrath* its sweep and cadence, they also accentuate its major flaw, Steinbeck's failure to integrate fully the modes of journalism and literature.

Too often his "general" chapters are simplistic editorials, haranguing the reader with dire prophecy, crude analysis, and cryptophilosophy that the "particular" chapters cannot sustain. Too often, as well, his fictional characters are mouthpieces for grandiose ideas, stereotypes that speak in "folk" lingo or stand as rigid symbols of portentous ritual. Yet Steinbeck believed that his documentary sources would give him a great living story, and he was not wrong. Despite its melodrama and bombast, the novel endures by drawing strength from its origins. At one moment, the book even reflects on this process of creation: "And it came about in the camps along the roads, on the ditch banks beside the streams, under the sycamores, that the story teller grew into being, so that the people gathered in the low firelight to hear the gifted ones. And they listened while the tales were told, and their participation made the stories great" (444).

That vision of art in the service of others captures the novel's deepest conviction, that between the general and particular lie undissolvable bonds. For all its rough-hewn quality the Joad family remains a collective unit, able to function best when sharing thought and labor. Their trials on the road and in squatter camps simply enlarge that principle, as adversity binds families with neighbors, turning migrants into a nomadic people: "In the evening a strange thing happened: the twenty families became one family, the children were the children of all. The loss of home became one loss, and the golden time in the West was one dream" (264). Gradually the Joad family dwindles in size. Elders die, sons drift away, infants come and go. Each of these losses impels the survivors toward a larger sense of union, beyond their original clan and tribe. At the end Jim Casy and Tom Joad may be gone, but they have passed a legacy of communion to Ma. After the stillbirth she tells Mrs. Wainwright, "Use' ta be the fambly was fust. It ain't so now. It's anybody. Worse off we get, the more we got to do" (606). That idea passes from mother to daughter, then takes an incarnate form when Rose of Sharon gives her breast to a stranger.

In working toward that final scene, conceived so early in his imagination, Steinbeck himself struggled through a long gestatory process that often threatened to abort or end in stillbirth. Along the way, many of his attitudes toward sexual and familial roles evolved, altering his sense of the project's identity. His early vision of documentary as an act of coalescence, a shared alliance through selfless communion, was naïve and adolescent, attributing greater dialectical and collaborative powers to Lange, Collins, Bristol, or Lorentz than they actually possessed. At the same time Steinbeck denied their spirit of cooperation by insisting on an image of artistry as stereotypically masculine. He believed that his father "liked the complete ruthlessness of my design to be a writer in spite of mother and hell" (W140), and that meant that a strong male writer would choose literature over journalism, individual effort over collaboration. Hence his decisions to work alone, yet the process of writing this novel proved to be mysterious and often humbling.

For in a large measure the book grew by itself, independent of his will or control. His creative process was strongly visual, aided by pictures and the work diary, which shifted him from a narrow "I" back to a broad, encompassing "We," the source of epic narrative. In the end, Steinbeck came to see that his creativity rose from both internal and external forces, not all of which he could control. His scenes of procreation and nurture bear the subtle imprint of authorial reflexion. He had not yet fathered children himself, but Rose of Sharon became his opportunity to imagine birth through another, one of the opposite gender. That final image of a mother nursing an old man ends the novel appropriately. As Steinbeck told his editor, the closing incident "must be an accident, it must be a stranger, and it must be quick. . . . The fact that the Joads don't know him, don't care about him, have no ties to him – that is the emphasis. The giving of the breast has no more sentiment than the giving of a piece of bread" (L178). The anonymous stranger feeds to survive, just as his author succeeds in delivering a story "which is so much greater than I" (W36), fiction that melded idea and fact, invention and reporting. That recognition suggests that *The Grapes of Wrath* endures as literature because it sprang from journalism, a strong and vibrant mother.

## NOTES

Parenthetical and abbreviated references are to:

B   Jackson J. Benson, *The True Adventures of John Steinbeck, Writer* (New York: Viking, 1984)

L   *Steinbeck: A Life in Letters,* eds. Elaine Steinbeck and Robert Wallsten (New York: Viking, 1975)

W   *Working Days: The Journals of* The Grapes of Wrath, ed. Robert DeMott (New York: Viking, 1989)
     John Steinbeck, *The Grapes of Wrath: Text and Criticism,* ed. Peter Lisca (New York: Viking, 1972)

1. A summary of critical responses to the last scene appears in Jules Chametzky, "The Ambivalent Endings of *The Grapes of Wrath,*" *Modern Fiction Studies* 11 (Spring, 1965), 34–44.
2. The best survey of Steinbeck as social novelist is David P. Peeler, *Hope among Us Yet* (Athens, GA: University of Georgia Press, 1987), 156–65. For his place in esthetic tradition, see John H. Timmerman, *John Steinbeck's Fiction* (Norman, OK: University of Oklahoma Press, 1986), 3–41.
3. Other references appear throughout Robert DeMott, *Steinbeck's Read-*

*ing* (New York: Garland, 1984), and Tetsumaro Hayashi, *A New Steinbeck Bibliography* (Metuchen, NJ: The Scarecrow Press, 1973).

4. Joseph Henry Jackson, "Why Steinbeck Wrote *The Grapes of Wrath,*" *Booklets for Bookmen* 1 (1940), 8–10. For summaries of the novel's reception see Peter Lisca's edition of *The Grapes of Wrath,* 695–707, and David Wyatt's Introduction to this volume. James Boylan, "Publicity for the Great Depression," in *Mass Media between the Wars,* Catherine L. Covert and John D. Stevens, eds. (Syracuse, NY: Syracuse University Press, 1984), 170.

5. William Stott, *Documentary Expression and Thirties America* (New York: Oxford University Press, 1973), 119; see also Alfred Kazin, *On Native Grounds* (New York: Harcourt, Brace, 1942; rpt. 1956), 382–98; and Karin Ohrn, *Dorothea Lange and the Documentary Tradition* (Baton Rouge, LA: Louisiana State University Press, 1980). For a poststructuralist concept of documentary fiction, see Barbara Foley, *Telling the Truth* (Ithaca, NY: Cornell University Press, 1986), a book that unaccountably excludes Steinbeck.

   Considerations of post-1930s literary journalism appear in Ronald Weber, *The Reporter as Artist* (New York: Hastings House, 1974); *The John McPhee Reader,* William Howarth, ed. (New York: Farrar, Straus, and Giroux, 1976); John Hollowell, *Fact and Fiction* (Chapel Hill, NC: University of North Carolina Press, 1977); Ronald Weber, *The Literature of Fact* (Athens, OH: Ohio University Press, 1980); John Hellman, *Fables of Fact* (Urbana, IL: University of Illinois Press, 1981); *The Literary Journalists,* ed. Norman Sims (New York: Ballantine Books, 1984); Shelley Fisher Fishkin, *From Fact to Fiction* (Baltimore, MD: Johns Hopkins University Press, 1985); Howard Good, *Acquainted with the Night* (Metuchen, NJ: Scarecrow Press, 1986); and Chris Anderson, *Style as Argument* (Carbondale, IL: Southern Illinois University Press, 1987).

6. Often called "intercalary" or "inter" chapters, but Steinbeck's terms "general" and "particular" are clearer. See Lisca's edition of *The Grapes of Wrath,* 731–2. Although critics have long known that Steinbeck used documentary sources, they assume such materials mainly affected his "general" chapters. For an example, see Joseph Fontenrose, *John Steinbeck* (New York: Barnes and Noble, 1963), 69.

7. Some of Steinbeck's antibourgeois attitudes probably expressed his rebellion against a middle-class background. See James Woodress, "John Steinbeck: Hostage to Fortune," *South Atlantic Quarterly* LXIII (Summer, 1964), 386.

8. Bristol's recollections and pictures appear in *Steinbeck* (Fall, 1988), 6–

8; David Roberts, "Travels with Steinbeck," *American Photographer* 22 (March, 1989), 45–8; and Jack Kelley, "Travels with Steinbeck," *People* (April 24, 1989), 67–74. The articles all differ on key points of evidence and emphasis.

9. Kelley, p. 73. Time, Inc. did not ignore the California labor migrants; see the unsigned "I Wonder Where We Can Go Now," *Fortune* (April, 1939), reprinted in the Lisca edition, 625–42. This forceful, well-researched article appeared just before publication of *The Grapes of Wrath*.

10. Kelley, p. 73.

11. Reporting accurately on migrants was difficult because they were transient and wary of strangers. Steinbeck also faced the ethical problem of writing about poverty without patronizing its victims. For a moving statement on this quandary, see Robert Coles, "James Agee's Search," *Raritan* (Summer, 1983), 74–100.

12. Lange's pictures – of migrant families, roadside scenes, and government camps – appeared in all but the seventh installment, which contained Steinbeck's stern denunciation of "Fascism in California." A full account of the Steinbeck–Collins relation is Jackson J. Benson, "To Tom, Who Lived It: John Steinbeck and the Man from Weedpatch," *Journal of Modern Literature* (April, 1976), 151–94. See also B359–63.

13. Stott, 58–63. For background on FSA photography, see Jack F. Hurley, *Portrait of a Decade* (Baton Rouge, LA: Louisiana State University Press, 1972); Penelope Dixon, *Photographers of the Farm Security Administration* (New York: Garland, 1983); and Pete Daniel, *Official Images* (Washington, DC: Smithsonian Institution, 1987). Studies of Lange include Karin Ohrn, *Dorothea Lange and the Documentary Tradition* (Baton Rouge, LA: Louisiana State University Press, 1980); Jefferson Hunter, *Image and Word* (Cambridge, MA: Harvard University Press, 1987), 88–102; and Carol Shloss, *In Visible Light* (New York: Oxford University Press, 1987), 201–29. Steinbeck wrote affectionately to Lange not long before her death in 1965; see *Steinbeck* (Summer, 1989), 6–7.

14. Stott, p. 59; Wendy Kozol, "Madonnas of the Fields: Photography, Gender, and 1930s Farm Relief," *Genders* 2 (July 1988), 17. See also "Photographic Contrivance" in Hunter, 99–105. *Their Blood Is Strong* closed with an epilogue, dated "Spring – 1938," that described Steinbeck's recent experiences at Visalia: "And then in the rains, with insufficient food, the children develop colds because the ground in the tents is wet. . . . I talked to a girl with a baby and offered her a

cigarette. She took two puffs and vomited in the street. She was ashamed. She shouldn't have tried to smoke, she said[,] for she hadn't eaten for two days. I heard a man whimpering that the baby was sucking but nothing came out of the breast. . . . Must the hunger become anger and the anger fury before anything will be done?"

15. Joseph R. Millichap, *Steinbeck and Film* (New York: Ungar, 1983), p. 29.

16. For a partial reprint of *Life* (June 5, 1939) see Arthur P. Moella, *FDR: The Intimate Presidency* (Washington, DC: Smithsonian Institution, 1982), p. 64.

17. Mark Twain's epigram appears in *Following the Equator* (1897), as the headnote to Chapter 15. For the genres of documentary, see John Puckett, *Five Photo-Textual Documentaries from the Great Depression* (Ann Arbor, MI: University of Michigan Research Press, 1984); also Stott on "Documentary NonFiction," 141–238; Hunter on "Collaborations," 33–64; and Peeler on "Traveling Reporters," 13–56.

18. David Wyatt suggests that ownership eventually became a divisive force in Steinbeck's first marriage. See *The Fall into Eden* (New York: Cambridge University Press, 1986), 154. Steinbeck was no slouch at business; when looking for a new publisher, he told his agent "Get a [Dun and] Bradstreet report on whoever you pick. All things else being equal, pick the one who makes the highest offer" (L169).

19. Susan Sontag, *On Photography* (New York: Farrar, Straus, and Giroux, 1978), 69. Years later, Bristol identified this portrait as the model for Rose of Sharon, "the character we had photographed together in the flooded boxcars of Visalia." See Bristol, p. 6.

20. Ulrich Keller, *The Highway as Habitat* (Santa Barbara, CA: University Art Museum, 1986), 29–32.

21. Millichap, 1–7, summarizes Steinbeck's relation to 1930s films.

22. Pare Lorentz, *The River* (New York: Stackpole Sons, 1938). This published text, subtitled "A National Drama in Pictures and Sound," includes many still photographs from FSA files.

23. Steinbeck was often attacked for *not* having described typical events or people, however. See Frank J. Taylor, "California's *Grapes of Wrath*," *Forum* 102 (November, 1939), 232–8; reprinted in the Lisca edition, 643–56.

24. Millichap, 32–8.

25. McWilliams defended Steinbeck as an accurate reporter in "California Pastoral," *Antioch Review* 2 (March, 1942), 103–21; reprinted in the Lisca edition, 657–79.

26. *The Forgotten Village* (New York: Viking Press, 1941), 6–7.

# 5

# The Artful Propaganda of Ford's
# *The Grapes of Wrath*

LESLIE GOSSAGE

A THOUGH audiences still want to see John Ford's *The Grapes of Wrath* (1940) — the film is available from Twentieth Century-Fox in 16-mm and 35-mm film, and in an inexpensive video — it has been belittled by critics since the emergence of scholarly interest in American film in the 1960s. Pauline Kael remembers it as "embarrassingly sentimental."[1] Andrew Sarris called it "New Dealish propaganda [that] . . . has dated badly."[2] Ford biographers expected better control from the master craftsman. Scholars of film adaptations of novels emphasize its flaws and the compromises of the text made by screenwriter Nunnally Johnson and producer Daryl F. Zanuck. Yet, when it came out, it was acclaimed. The film was chosen as best picture for 1940 by both the National Board of Review and the New York Film Critics. Jane Darwell won an Oscar for her performance as Ma Joad. For his direction, John Ford received both the Oscar and an award from the New York Film Critics. Of the film *Life* magazine said, "bitter, authentic, honest, it marches straight to its tragic end."[3] *The New York Times* critic Frank Nugent, who had denigrated Zanuck's films so often that Twentieth Century-Fox had pulled its advertising from the *Times*, placed *Grapes* on the "one small uncrowded shelf devoted to cinema's masterworks."[4] The man most likely to have noticed the detrimental effects of Hollywood on *Grapes*, Steinbeck himself, wrote in praise of the film to his agent Elizabeth Otis, December 15, 1939:

> We went down in the afternoon and that evening saw *Grapes* at Twentieth Century. Zanuck has more than kept his word. He has a hard, straight picture in which the actors are submerged so completely that it looks and feels like a documentary film and certainly it has a hard, truthful ring. No punches were pulled — in fact with

descriptive matter removed, it is a harsher thing than the book, by
far. (L195)[5]

In the 1950s he praised it again in the same terms in a letter to
Henry Fonda (L603). The vast majority of contemporary reviews
were favorable, yet by the 1960s the film was described as either
sentimental, propagandistic, or insufficiently realistic, with the no-
table exception of James Agee. In a 1942 essay in the *Nation*, he
said that, even though he respected John Ford, he disliked most of
*The Grapes of Wrath*. In a 1943 review of *The Human Comedy*, he
wrote, about the acting style in it and *Grapes*, that "when there is
any pretense whatever of portraying 'real' people . . . such actors
are painfully out of place."[6]

Why is there so much disagreement about what this film actually "looks and feels" like? In the first place, critics' tastes change
as their perceptions of audience change. The critics of the 1960s
detested sentimental manipulation in cinema, and perhaps also
expected current audiences to be more politically and socially liberal than the audience for whom *Grapes* was filmed. These prescriptive beliefs about the relation of art to audience made *Grapes*
seem more dated during a 1960s or early 1970s viewing than it
does today. The re-emergence of the political Right, empowered by
a populace who have rekindled beliefs in hollow patriotism, in the
nuclear family, fundamentalist Christianity, and the righteousness
of laissez faire capitalism, gives *Grapes* an audience today similar to
the audiences of the late 1930s, when Depression-era radicalism
was quickly waning. Many of our most pressing and yet ignored
social and economic problems – the homelessness of whole families, the cutting of social programs, the influx of immigrants and
migration of natives to areas that will not accommodate them, the
devouring of small businesses by megabusinesses, and an agricultural system that once again needs new techniques and man-
agement to keep farmers and the land from disaster – echo conditions that brought about the writing and filming of *Grapes*. So *The
Grapes of Wrath*, both novel and film, should be returned to the
canon.

In the second place, the film of *Grapes* has received short shrift in
academic cinema studies perhaps because critics have been unset-

tled by the film's unusual conflation of sentimental fiction and documentary references. But it is this striking mix of documentary cues and powerful storytelling that has continuously drawn audiences in spite of the serious editing flaws (what happened to Noah?) and the film's unavoidable and unfortunate diminution of Steinbeck's documentary epic. This chapter examines the way in which the film connects art experience and life experience for the audience by manipulating the tension between social commentary, presented through documentary references, and character identification, which is established through the use of literary and cinematic conventions.

Admittedly, much is lost from Steinbeck's work in Nunnally Johnson's script for Ford's film. The self-imposed Production Code of Hollywood joined with the faintly liberal politics of the filmmakers to erase the elaborate connections that Steinbeck develops between the private and the public – the lure of domination: the challenges of a woman hunted down or of an immense tract of land bought and paid for. Because of the Production Code and probably also because of their own sexual politics, the filmmakers could not include the farmyard jokes and anecdotes that in the novel so often express the inherent violence of patriarchal ownership – the desire to control land, animals, and women. They could not show the domestic violence at work in the changing relationship of Ma and Pa. They could not include Al's tomcatting and Tom's rebuke of him for it. They could not let us see the details of Rose of Sharon and Connie's intimate relationship, nor her starved pregnancy, nor the enigmatic act of communal piety that ends Steinbeck's plot. Giving her breast to a starving tenant farmer creates an analogy between the personal and the political. Rose of Sharon and the farmer have both been abandoned by hierarchical powers – husband and corporate landowner. These powers have withheld the sustenance and security owed to wife and tenant for their subservience, their willingness to work, and the expected product of their labor. If either of them realizes that the patriarchal system itself is to blame and deserves destroying, the wine of rebellion will be served round. Steinbeck's novel suggests that the rapaciousness of human nature toward agricultural land and toward fellow beings is to blame for the socioeconomic crisis of

103

farming in 1930s America, but the film touches on this constellation of ideas essentially not at all. In fact, the film's disclaimer prologue blames the weather.

Nonetheless, the film is a clear primer about the hard realities of day labor. Tom's understanding of the economics of his family's situation comes piecemeal from Muley and Casy and others; we absorb it as he does. Despite the prologue, the text of the film clearly aims an accusing finger at the banks and land companies unwilling to help the people who have worked the companies' lands for decades. We feel the indignant frustration of Muley and his son when they cannot find a human being to hold morally responsible for the disaster: "Well, who *do* we shoot?!" When the Joads find work we see them underpaid at the end of the day and overcharged at the company store. When the strike is broken, the scabs, the Joads among them, must take a fifty-percent cut in pay per box of peaches, just as Casy predicted. The Joads will now work all day for the same money that they had earned yesterday when they started work at midday. If yesterday's supper, bought with a half-day's earnings, left them hungry, there is no hope of eating adequately on the new lower pay. Their plan eventually to earn enough to buy a modest piece of land with a small white house seems more and more improbable. The film progresses relentlessly to the conclusion that Tom reaches under Casy's tutelage: Striking is the only way to struggle for their rights as human beings. The film realistically points out the greatest obstacle to a strike – the breadwinner's concern for the welfare of his own family. Granted that the film does not offer solutions to this conflict, it does show that the protagonist has become a zealot of workers' rights and intends to go off to try to find some solutions. In this way the film is politically radical, and belies the sentimental speech that Zanuck put in Ma's mouth as the last word of the film. Ma may think she should stay in her place, but the film's text has developed a radical rejection of this in Tom's character. *Grapes* stands near the beginning of a tradition of labor films including *On the Waterfront, Blue Collar, Norma Rae, Silkwood, Matewan,* and *Eight Men Out.*

In *Novels into Film* George Bluestone's criticisms of the film as an adaptation that weakened the radical politics of the book depend mainly on the filmmakers' omissions of radical speeches, their omission of events, and their rearrangement of the plot.[7] While it is undeniable that political statements in the dialogue have been softened and that the plot rearrangement matches a more sanguine view of New Deal progress, Bluestone's argument glosses over the power of the shocking imagery of the film. There is nothing soft or easy about the scene of eight or ten children scrambling over a refuse pile to find tin cans because "a lady's gonna feed us!" No punches are pulled when the stranger in the first camp at which the Joads stop describes the deaths of his children – "Coroner wrote down they died of heart failure. Heart failure?! And their little bellies all swelled out like pig bladders?!" After a woman is accidentally shot in the Hooverville by the "authorities," the close-up of the elderly lady who holds the limp, moaning victim and says to the cop, "this woman's bleeding to death," is especially shocking and powerful because she is a stranger to us and yet her face and words are so moving. The razing of Muley's house by bulldozer, the deaths of Grampa and Granma, the murderous mob that attacks the Joads' truck, and the murders of Casy and his murderer, all contribute to the hard edges of this film. This is a world where people, good people, die of starvation, exposure, and abuse by the authorities; it is not the cleaned-up, poetically just world of Hollywood drama. The cramped and dilapidated interior of the Joads' quarters at the Keene (Hooper, in the novel) ranch and the shanties of the Hooverville shockingly express the degrading transformation of farm tenants into harvest migrants.

Besides this shocking imagery, certain other strategies of Ford's style, and perhaps of cinematographer Gregg Toland's also, conspire in *The Grapes of Wrath* to prevent a distancing pity and to create respectful sympathy. In *The Implied Reader*, Wolfgang Iser contends that "the overlapping of different forms makes it possible to communicate the unknown through the known, which brings about the expansion of our experience."[8] The mixing of genres that Iser refers to is exactly what the filmmakers of *Grapes* attempt by juxtaposing expressionist and newsreel styles, by combining sentimental conventions of characterization with documentary cues of realistic atmosphere and open-ended plot, and by fuelling the conflict in the viewer between seeing oneself as sentimental art consumer versus implicated citizen. To say that Hollywood cinema is manipulative is an understatement, but to applaud the power and complication of that manipulation in this case may strike readers as morally or esthetically corrupt. Manipulation of a free and thinking viewer can lead to knowledge. I agree with G. B. Shaw that "All great Art and Literature is propaganda" (Preface to *On the Rocks*).

> I wish to boast that *Pygmalion* has been an extremely successful play . . . It is so intensely and deliberately didactic, and its subject is esteemed so dry, that I delight in throwing it at the heads of the wiseacres who repeat the parrot cry that art should never be didactic. It goes to prove my contention that art should never be anything else. (Preface to *Pygmalion*)

Though manipulation is often pejoratively called propaganda, the opposite of didactic manipulation is in fact an unchallenging reassurance that acts as propaganda for the status quo. As novelist and filmmaker Lynne Tillman has written,

> What's called propaganda is always the philosophy and information different from that which is held by those in power. History is working with and constructing meaning(s), and power depends on the ability to define and impose meaning. And since everything we do operates out of a politic, even when a maker might think not, all work can be considered propaganda.[9]

Steinbeck came to trust screenwriter Nunnally Johnson not to betray the book, but he also threatened Zanuck, by putting in escrow the sum that he received for screen rights to the book so that he could sue Zanuck if the final cut watered down the facts and situations of the screenplay.[10] In the end, the filmmakers do seem to have been concerned with the task of making the movie-going public understand the nature and needs of the migrants – a task made difficult, perhaps even impossible, by the bourgeois prejudices and vested interests of that public. A combination of manipulative techniques culled from familiar genres was the solution they came to.

Ford's film follows one of Steinbeck's intentions in *The Grapes of Wrath:* The camera eye, like the narrative voice of the novel, moves back and forth between the points of view of the migrants and those who are distanced from them by economic class and by experience. Rose of Sharon's final desperate act of work, with all its tensions of communal feeling and unnatural sexuality, accuses the reader of ignorant selfishness. By the absence of charitable middle-class people in his novel, Steinbeck silently accused America of complacency about the hundreds of thousands of migrants starving along the road. Chapter 15 contains the only bit of help to be offered the Joads by a person of a higher economic class, and yet even that scene is presented cynically, since what Mae and Al donate, they more than regain from the truck drivers' tips.[11] The short-lived and superficial curiosity about the "Okies" expressed by Mae and the truck drivers demonstrates the great distance, ignorance, and misunderstanding between middle-class America and the dispossessed of the farming country. The self-absorbed businessman and his wife, whom Mae categorizes in the novel as "shitheels," are even more oblivious to the migrants' plight. Shitheels are people who treat Mae like shit – forging a longer chain of condescension and hateful distancing. They can't put themselves in others' shoes, like Casy can. Steinbeck extends the artistic act of imaginative identification into life experience in Tom's final speech. The film also works with this sort of identification, moving methodically toward that speech. For the most part Ford, like Steinbeck, was making his story for an audience that not only rarely included migrants, but may even have been hostile or condescending to them. Demonstrating the strength, independence, dignity, intelligence – the humanity – of these dispossessed people was Steinbeck's aim and that of the writers, photographers, and journalists from 1935 to the end of the Depression years, who reacted against an exploitation of tenant farmers in sentimental forms of art and journalism.

In his *Documentary Expression and Thirties America,*[12] William Stott has given us a critical history of the documentary book genre which informed and inspired Steinbeck's novel and Ford's film. The sharecropper was the most prevalent subject for these sentimentally polemical books of photographs with texts. The most popular one – *You Have Seen Their Faces* (released November 1937) – was photographed by Margaret Bourke-White and written by Erskine Caldwell from their travels through southern states in the summer of 1936. Although there is evidence that Caldwell humbly respected the farmers while traveling among them, Stott tells us that

> Caldwell himself did the tenants violence in his text, disparaged their lives and possessions – but he did so because he knew his readers would and knew that to convince them otherwise would take enormous imaginative labor on his part and theirs and undermine his polemical purpose. About farm tenancy his text made the "usual liberal complaint," as George Elliott thinks it: "How awful this is. Aren't you ashamed that you let fellow Americans live like this?" That was the message his audience expected; indeed, the popularity of *You Have Seen Their Faces* lends weight to Robert Warshow's belief that the tendency of mass culture is to eliminate the "moral content of experience, putting in its place a system of conventionalized 'responses.' " But so conventional a text as Caldwell's would never have sold had his book not offered something new on the sharecropper photographs. *You Have Seen Their Faces* was called the *Uncle Tom's Cabin* of tenant farming, and Norman Cousins said it would deserve the credit "if all the talk about the share-cropper's plight is ever translated into action," thanks to Bourke-White.[13]

A self-consciousness about exploitation and propaganda arose among the serious artists and social scientists of the time. Stott tells us that some subsequent docubooks – H. C. Nixon's *Forty Acres and Steel Mules* (1938), Paul Taylor and Dorothea Lange's *An American Exodus* (1939), and, of course, James Agee and Walker Evans's *Let Us Now Praise Famous Men* (1941) – criticized *You Have Seen Their Faces* directly in their texts and indirectly through their methods.[14] Steinbeck had destroyed his first attempt at a novel about the migrants – "L'Affaire Lettuceberg" (B348) – although as he was writing it he described it to Elizabeth Otis, May 2, 1938, in these terms: "It is written not for intellectuals at all but for people who make up vigilance committees. . . . It is a mean, nasty book and if I could make it nastier I would" (B375–6, this excerpt not available in *A Life in Letters*). He finally chose instead to express his anger at the oppressors by centering on the admirable qualities he had witnessed in the oppressed, creating a humanistic docu-epic novel instead of an authorially dominated docusatire. The public had been treated repeatedly to analytical tracts in favor of changing the tenants' conditions, as well as to sentimentalized representations of the migrant farmers as pitiable characters drawn to create an effect. He chose instead, like Taylor and Lange and Evans and Agee, to express his impressions of how they really were from his experiences among them.

In the documentary tradition, it is difficult to walk a solid line between the audience's sentimental expectations and the artist's goal to bring new insight to that audience, while not exploiting the subjects of inquiry. In an era filled with pathetic views of the Depression's victims, Ford's film worked with audience expectations in order to sell itself but succeeded in avoiding the maudlin sentimentality that masquerades as fellow feeling. *The Grapes of Wrath* is a two-faced film – it looks squarely at the migrants' reality that Steinbeck wrote about in a radical frame of mind, but it also nods at the conservative powers that be. In *Theory of Film*, Siegfried Kracauer points to Steinbeck's novel as particularly cinematic in its narrative methods, and in doing so uses *Grapes* as an example of the political potential of film:

> [Steinbeck's novel] exposes the predicament of the migratory farm workers, thus revealing and stigmatizing abuses in our society. This . . . falls into line with the peculiar potentialities of film. In recording and exploring physical reality, the cinema virtually challenges us to confront that reality with the notions we commonly entertain about it – notions which keep us from perceiving it. Perhaps part of the medium's significance lies in its revealing powers.[15]

Ford's *Grapes* does aim to reveal facts that will change notions held by those who would deny the humanity of the migrants. What Kracauer neglects in making this sanguine assertion, however, is that the *concealing* power of cinema is often as strong as its "revealing power," because cinema, even documentary cinema, is a *creation* of a physical reality, not an unmediated recording of reality. Creation implies an author who shapes and omits, frames and edits "facts." Certainly, much factual information from the novel that might radicalize the viewer is omitted from the film, yet the power of story works well in Ford's film to move the viewer. The camera negotiates with the audience to gain sympathy, but not pity, for the Joads and their kin of the road. The film of *Grapes* tries to create a radical continuum between identification with characters in art and active sympathy with the Other in life.

In his biography of John Ford, Tag Gallagher points out that "We are led to identify with 'Our People' (as Ma Joad puts it) and to regard the rest of the world as alien. Such a process of identification/alienation is essentially revolutionary."[16] But, without developing this idea, he goes on to agree with other critics that the "thrust of the film's 'politics' of empathy and alienation . . . is deflected in plot development."[17] When we examine the development of identification in the film closely, we discover a tension between *alien views* and *involved views,* one that makes the migrants a powerful source of political meaning that overrides easy sentimentality.

At the beginning of the film, Tom Joad is presented as a mysterious and threatening character. The filmmakers play on the audience's fear of convicts and vagrants. The film begins with alien views of Tom and works towards identification with him very slowly: Until the sequence with Muley, there are no close-ups that ask us to give him special sympathetic attention. The film opens with an alien view of Tom in long shot, coming up to a crossroads eatery, a black form except for his white cap, the shadow of which obscures his face. He silently waits and watches by a truck as the truck driver dallies with a waitress. As Tom leans on the truck in the foreground, the truck driver appears as a much smaller form in between the truck and Tom's body – in the crook of his arm. This shot helps to make Tom seem threatening, as does his verbal manipulation of the driver in the next shot. Within the truck Tom and the driver are still shown in two-shots, neither looking at the other, while the driver pries into Tom's past. When Tom gets fed up with the driver's nosiness – "Gotta trade?" – Tom turns toward the driver, slowly, the new stiff cap in profile becoming a threatening beak. Tom challenges the driver to ask what he really wants to know. "Why don't you get at it, buddy?" Soon after, still in the same medium two-shot, Tom says that his road is coming up. As Tom gets out of the truck and finishes his hostile conversation with the driver, Ford presents this sequence in alternating point-of-view shots that begin to create the tension of alien versus involved views. First, Ford distances the audience for a moment with an extreme long shot of Tom leaving the truck: a low-angle shot that shows the dry and chunky field dirt by the roadside. In this distancing shot Tom is a tiny anonymous hitchhiker being dropped off. Then we get a shot from behind Tom's back as he holds the door open and says to the frightened driver: "You're about to bust a gut to know what I done, ain't ya?" Then we get reverse point-of-view shots. From Tom's point of view there follows a medium close-up of the driver's frightened face; he doesn't answer. Then a shot of what the driver sees: Tom's threatening, joking face in a medium shot that includes the black arch of the door frame: "Well, I ain't a guy to let you down (pause) it was home-a-side," says Tom, punctuating his declaration with a slam of the cab door. Then we get a shot from Tom's point of view of the frightened driver in the cab as the truck pulls away. These point-of-view shots set up the tension in the viewer between a desire to identify with this fictional sharecropper and a recognition that in his own life the viewer, on the opposite side of the socioeconomic fence, would find Tom frightening.

Besides the extreme long shot of Tom as an anonymous hitch-hiker that interrupts the intense dialogue with the truck driver, there are other alien views of the Joads that contrast with involved views of them as protagonists. After the viewer has gotten to know the whole family and has been involved in their excited reunion with Tom, these involved views are interrupted by the arrival of the superintendent's car, seen against the fields and distant low hills, in a long shot from the family's point of view, as the superintendent honks and yells, "Joad! John Joad!" The next shot is striking in its abrupt distancing of the viewer from the Joads. It is an alien view of the family in the yard walking toward the car – a disorganized, uncomposed long shot in which they look bedraggled and forlorn. From the point of view of the arriving car, this long shot reminds the viewer of his alienation in real life from people in circumstances like the Joads. The shot seems candid or documentary in style for a moment, but as the Joads walk toward the car, they form a tableau of family in front of the house and the truck; thus, this alien view ends with a reminder of our recent involved views of them.

A similar interruption of narrative identification occurs in the earlier sequence in the dark, empty Joad house. The viewer's sympathetic involvement with Tom and Muley is continuous in the sequence except for an interrupting alien view that implicates the viewer. To begin Muley's memory sequence – "A man come one day . . . " – Ford chose not Muley's point of view, but the view from the back seat of the superintendent's car. This throws the viewer into an alien view of Muley's family for a moment. The reverse point-of-view shot from where Muley stands listening shows us the superintendent through the car's windshield. So, again, reverse point-of-view shots set up a tension in viewers between distance and sympathy – between our condition in life experience and our condition in art experience.

The camera eye does not look at Tom in close-up until we are far into the film. The long sequence of meeting Casy and philosophizing with him is shot in medium, three-quarter, and full shots. Ford saved the first close-up to make it an emphatically involved view. After Tom has looked around in his parents' house by candlelight, picking up belongings, describing them for Casy, we see Tom in a slightly low-angle medium shot, alone in the frame, his hand and face lit by the candle. Ford, who rarely uses moving camera at all in this film, suddenly moves the camera in and tilts up to create a low-angle close-up of Tom's half-lit face as he asks, "Reckon they're dead?" This emotional camera movement and resulting close-up begins the involved views of Tom and Muley that take place in the dark Joad house.

The first part of Muley's memory sequence ends in a dissolve from Muley's dark figure squatting in the blowing white dust to an extreme close-up of Tom's concerned face surrounded by pitch black. The dissolve is a visual representation of character identification – Tom seems to take Muley's memory inside him. Tom, the outsider like us, has become deeply involved with another's story; he feels the trouble as if it could happen to him. Tom's willingness to put himself in Muley's shoes provides a standard against which the audience is expected to measure the responses of the people encountered by the Joads in their migration. Ford begins the truck-stop sequence from inside the diner before Pa, Ruthie, and Winfield come in, so that we can reflect on how we might feel about Pa if he were a stranger to us as he is to Mae and the drivers. The esthetic existence of these Joad characters is repeatedly linked by these distancing views to the political existence of their social group in relation to the social group that most viewers belong to.

112

By the time Ford allows the service-station attendants to voice the worst that might be lurking in the viewers' minds, the audience has become so involved with the Joad family that the commentary of the grease monkeys drives us still closer to the Joads.

Vivian C. Sobchack, among others, has argued that Ford meant to abstract the Joads from their sociopolitical milieu in order to make a universal story of a family struggling against adversity: The film "involved the contemporaneous viewer primarily on the level of sentiment, because its transcendent vision of the Joads as an archetypal family freed the viewer from the responsibility for specific social action."[18] Admittedly, Ford was no social activist or satirist, yet one must ignore major portions of the film in order to argue that the film is more about family than it is about the migrants' plight and their labor struggles. If the film is merely about a universalized struggling family, then why did Ford include the striking dialogue of the gas-station attendants that makes the viewer squirm and reflect on his or her own prejudices against people like the Joads? Well into the film, long after we have accepted the Joads as protagonists, the following dialogue reminds us that these protagonists are part of a large group, dispossessed not only of homes and jobs, but also of reputation. This treatment is especially undeserved as they enter the desert, crossed heroically by so many pioneers. The immaculate white suits of the glib, gum-chewing station attendants contrast remarkably with their nasty and ignorant commentary.

> "Holy Moses. What a hard-looking outfit!"
> "All them Okies is hard looking."
> "I'd hate to hit that desert in a jalopy like that."
> "You and me got sense. Them Okies got no sense and no feelings. They ain't human. A human couldn't live the way they do. A human being couldn't stand to be so miserable."
> "Just don't know any better, I guess."

Much of the film works to show the idiocy of these statements.

The drama of alienated or involved looking is rendered intensely in the sequence in which the Joads enter the Hooverville, because of the triangulation between the Joads, the campers, and the moviegoer looking. Ford and Toland set up the only extended moving-camera shot in the whole film for this documentary-style view of a fictional Hooverville and its inhabitants. The camera views the camp from the Joads' truck as the Joads inspect it. The moving-camera shot seems almost like newsreel footage; it is shot at an odd angle, slightly askew. The content of this shot is that of Farm Security Administration documentary photography: Raggedly dressed people, slow, tired, wary, some quite thin, pass before the truck. But they do something they cannot often do in FSA documentary photos: They stop to stare inquisitively at the Joads. The voyeurism is made uncomfortably reciprocal. The details are eloquent: black-smoking, rigged-up stove pipes; huts, shacks, and tents with varying measures taken to create privacy; a jalopy for sale; a man repairing a tire; a woman carrying junk wood for her fire; a woman washing clothes in a bucket; a woman protectively herding children out of the way of the truck. When the truck stops, we get a series of alternating shots of the observing Joads in the truck cab and of the people they are looking at. Six shots go by before a word is uttered. A very realistic shot of a toothless, emaciated couple in front of a hut is followed by a shot of Pa, John, Connie, and Casy on the back of the truck – a shot in which the Joads don't look much better off, yet Tom will break the silence two shots later by saying to Ma, "Sure do look none too prosperous. Should we go somewheres else?" The Joads are having an alien view of "Okies," just as the viewer has been implicated in having alien views of the Joads. As Tom utters these words, trying futilely to see the campers as different/separate from his own family, the filmmakers have made visible in the windshield a reflection of a Hooverville woman looking at them, in order to assert the reciprocity/mutuality of looking in order to separate or identify.

The radical connection between looking at others and feeling for them is again powerfully expressed in the scene when Ma doesn't have enough stew for both her family and the camp children milling about the Joad tent. Uncle John, staring at the children, feigns a belly ache – "I ain't hongry" – and when Tom yells at him to get in the tent and eat, John says under his breath, "It wouldn't be no use: I'd still see them in the tent." His absorption of this visual experience, an involved view, is meant to mimic or prescribe the viewer's relation to the Joads and to the campers through looking.

By mixing expressionist narrative techniques with documentary cues and content, Ford keeps fiction and reality in constructive connection. The dark, expressionist sequences assert the inner life of the characters, balancing the distancing effects inherent in the external, opaque views of documentary style. The authors of the docubooks in the mid-1930s felt that the audience needed captions giving voices to the pictured people. The presentation of inner life through quotation – whether invented by Caldwell for Bourke-White's *You Have Seen Their Faces* or recorded at the moment of the photo taking and carefully transcribed by Taylor and Lange for *An American Exodus* – was considered an important addition to the possibly alienating surface of the person photographed. Through artistic conventions of narrative, Ford's film presents the inner lives of migrant characters so that the viewer, however prejudiced against the migrants' appearance, must admit having thoughts, concerns, and feelings in common with them.

Muley's memory sequence presents the blending of contrasting expressionist and documentary approaches. Tom Collins, the camp director of the actual Weedpatch camp and fellow traveler with Steinbeck among the migrants, received $15,000 to be technical advisor to the filmmakers. The realism of the documentary details in the film are probably owing in great part to his contributions, as well as to Pare Lorentz's docufilms, *The Plow That Broke the Plains* and *The River*. Ford uses darkness in his expressionist sequences to evoke the contents of the mind – Tom walks around in his parents' house remembering. Muley begins telling his three-part story in the dark, but the story is brightly sunlit and in high contrast. Since high-contrast shooting was not common in Hollywood style in the 1930s, the viewer might easily associate that high-contrast look with the documentary photographs so common in books and photomagazines of the time. Muley knows about the economic facts of the evictions, so his speech also combines the emotional and the documentary. Muley is not an object acted on by document collectors, but a subject speaking, documenting his own story. The power of the sequence lies in the viewer seeing Muley from inside and outside at once. The only approach more powerful and true would be to have a migrant write and direct his own documentary narrative.

Ford alludes to the complex interior life of Ma Joad in the scene when she sorts her valued possessions. Sobchack asserts that these dramatic scenes framed by darkness abstract the characters from the socioeconomic milieu.[19] On the contrary, Ma is presented as both an expressionist character and a documentary personage. The objects that she examines, which we see in close-up, cue documentary associations because of their particularity: news clipping, postcard, World's Fair souvenir. This real woman lives in an historical moment. Yet the viewer becomes curious about the emotional meaning of these objects – we are alerted to the fact that Ma has an unelaborated personal history. The shot of her sad face reflected in the clouded mirror while she holds earrings to her earlobes is part of the universalized tradition handed down from German expressionism (through F. W. Murnau in Ford's case). This intensely psychological moment expresses Ma's inner life – her sense of beauty desired, time lost, hopes dashed, and identity embattled. This expression of inner life helps the viewer to understand and identify with Ma, and it asserts the human dignity and emotional complexity of the migrants for audiences familiar with the expressionist tradition, but unfamiliar – perhaps insistently so – with transients except as "eyesores" along the roadside. Tom's mental life is also expressed in dark expressionist sequences – in the first camp stop on the road, in the truck with Ma when the mob approaches them, with Casy talking strike strategy in the tent, and with Ma at the dance floor just before he leaves the family. By juxtaposing nightmarish expressionist scenes of emotional and intellectual content and dazzlingly daylit documentary-style views of the same characters, Ford and Toland pull off a double-pronged manipulation of the audience that steers the viewer away from the easy reassurance of sentimental Hollywood narrative.

Even the casting of Henry Fonda as Tom Joad also develops the tension between traditional story and documentary. Although Fonda is a matinee idol of sorts, he can make himself look tough and even frightening. His head viewed from certain angles can work against his Hollywood good looks. He knows how to use his jaw muscles and his teeth to appear threatening and alienating in close-ups that are usually intended to make a Hollywood star attractive. When Ma first sees Tom out in the yard at Uncle John's, for example, the close-up of Fonda, as he greets her with "Ma," is all teeth and hard pale eyes. It is not the sentimental scene one might expect. His beak of a cap and his short-tempered speech patterns also help undercut his star quality. Fonda's casting history included both American patriots and criminals – not only the title role in *Young Mr. Lincoln* (1939) and a pioneer in *Drums along the Mohawk* (1939), but also Frank James in *Jesse James* (1939) and an ex-con in *You Only Live Once* (1937). Casting Fonda as Tom helped identify the migrants – those frightening strangers – as fellow Americans. Reintegrating the migrants into the history of the American Dream seems to be an aim of *Grapes* as both novel and film, although the film is less willing than the novel to question the efficacy of the dream.

Biographer Jackson J. Benson contends that Steinbeck was "essentially" a "New Deal Democrat" (B371), yet the novel impugns capitalist farming in America more severely than a Roosevelt reformist would. In the novel, Steinbeck takes his attack on greedy ownership of land back through American history. While strong on the rights of labor, the film avoids attacks on ownership and only indirectly refers to the agricultural problems of depleted topsoil, mechanization of cultivation, and monocrop culture. The film illustrates the carrot of the American Dream of rags to riches while the novel shows it to be wrong-headed – sour grapes for the few who achieve it and ungraspable for the many. In the film Ford and Johnson added an Oklahoma native who came out two years earlier and made it in California – played by Ward Bond. He greets the Joads at their arrival in their first California town and then because of curfew laws he must advise them to move along out to the Hooverville. The Ward Bond character expresses the ambivalence of the "self-made" American toward the people he rose up from. Zanuck himself had come to Hollywood a poor boy from the edge of the Dust Bowl in the Midwest and had risen to be a top producer at Warner Brothers by the time talkies arrived. It seems to be a perverse sort of honesty about their own success that makes these filmmakers put a more sanguine face on the possibilities of making it in America. The filmmakers also present the Joads as Americans with a different past than Steinbeck gave them. Two of Ma's trinkets in the film have been added – the postcard of the

Statue of Liberty and the porcelain dog from the St. Louis Exposition. These trinkets add a connection to a broader part of America. Ma's relatives or friends had time and money to travel. Or they moved to places like New York City and started new lives. Steinbeck had presented the Joads as insulated and naïve in their barely populated farming county. The filmmakers, on the other hand, want to identify the Joads with the yearnings of the middle-class for upward mobility and traveling adventure. The Statue of Liberty on a postcard would speak subtly to every immigrant in the audience – the Joads are like you are or like you were when you first got here. John Ford himself may have chosen to add the postcard to allude to his own sort of background as an Irish immigrant who became a successful American. It would have been a kind of lie for Zanuck and Ford to present the American Dream as inoperable because they lived it, and yet, of course, for every Zanuck and Ford who made it, thousands failed to achieve even modest versions of their dreams. The filmmakers knew this and their political ambivalence about haves and have-nots shows at every turn.

The character that Ward Bond plays expresses this ambivalence most succinctly when he turns businesslike after greeting the Joads as fellow "Okies":

> What I gotta tell you is this: Don't park in town tonight. Just go right on out to that camp. If I catch you in town after dark, gotta lock you up.
> But what are we gonna do?
> Well, Pop, that just ain't up to me. I don't mind telling you the guy they oughta lock up is the guy who sent them things [the handbills advertising work] out.

It seems fair to guess that if the migrants had been Hispanic – as they are today (under similar housing conditions) – we wouldn't have heard about it nearly so loudly nor in epic form. Steinbeck and the filmmakers were concerned about these American migrants precisely because they were descendants of the yeoman farmers of Anglo-Saxon stock who had "tamed" both the Plains and the Native Americans who "roamed" there. That blacks from the tenant-farmed South were traveling Route 80 to the far West and were involved in farm workers' strikes (see *An American Exodus* and B303–4) mattered not for this story. That women struggled side by side with men not only in the fields and orchards but in the labor movements as well (for example, Caroline Decker, see B302ff and the excerpt from Steinbeck's letter quoted on B316, but omitted from *A Life in Letters*) mattered not. Steinbeck and the filmmakers who used his novel presented a traditional extended family of yeoman farmers, who, it is implied, deserved better than they received in part because of their genetic/cultural history rather than because they were human beings, every one of whom deserves food, shelter, and the chance to work to keep supplying the other two for his or her dependents. The filmmakers' implication, though unfortunately quite racist and culturally chauvinist, allowed for some richly seductive images of an imagined past, attractive probably even to the braceros and later the Chicanos who replaced the "Okies" in the fields – organizers for Cesar Chavez used Steinbeck's novel as part of their consciousness-raising campaign in the 1960s, aimed at American consumers (B423).

Ford's talent for iconographic tableaux is evident in many shots of farm environments and family circles. The first scene of the Joads is presented as a tableau of the farm kitchen table in which the extended family forms a circle of tow-headed or gray-thatched faces. Muley's family forms a tableau as his house is bulldozed. When the superintendent arrives to warn Uncle John to "be off by morning," the family arranges itself in an oval-to-circular composition. When Tom and Casy walk to Uncle John's, we are treated to a gorgeous sunrise silhouette of fences, farmhouse, and windmill. At the end of Muley's tale as he squats in the dust, he suddenly stops crying and looks off to the fields, creating the perfect icon representing the farmer waiting on and watching weather and crops. Ford is adept at myth making about the history of the yeoman farmer, omitting the equal, if not more influential, contributions to the creation of America by the unfree laborers at the bottom and the omnipresent and omnipotent corporations at the top.

While it is clearly documented that Steinbeck wrote purposely to get governmental help for the migrants, to reveal and thereby to end the clandestine abuse of them by the Associated Farmers and vigilantes, and to clear away dehumanizing impressions of the migrants' characters, it is not clear that anyone among the film-

119

makers, except perhaps Johnson, whom Steinbeck trusted (L186), was deeply committed to improving the migrants' conditions. What solutions did they propose in their version of *The Grapes of Wrath?* Perhaps they thought that reaching as many viewers as possible, by offering a film less "offensive" than the book, would serve the migrants by bringing attention to them that Congress could not ignore. The building of more government camps was at a standstill – only two had been completed while thousands of migrants continued to arrive in California. There is also a curious addition to the film that is not in the book: The Wheat Patch camp visually mimics a Native American village that we pass through when the Joads are on the road in Arizona. Perhaps Ford and Johnson wished to make an oblique reference to the dangerous possibility of genocide of the migrants, or perhaps this allusion to the peaceful village points to a nostalgic fantasy – a wish to start America over again. Today such a solution seems absurd, but in fact Roosevelt himself had the pipe dream of settling the migrants on arable land in the Columbia River Basin. In any case, the war changed the farm workers' population and their problems within the next two years, so we can never know what changes the film or the novel might have fostered.

The filmmakers' political commitment has often been measured against Steinbeck's by comparing the endings of the film and the book. Nunnally Johnson moved the government-camp episode (389ff), which is between the Hooverville and Hooper ranch (called Keene ranch in the film) episodes in the novel, to the end of the screenplay. He omitted the cotton-picking episode, the boxcar flood, and the final episode of the novel entirely. He has Tom leave the government camp instead of the boxcar camp. Tom's final speech in the novel (570–2) is condensed and delivered to Ma on the deserted dance floor rather than in the vine-covered cave where Tom hides in the novel. Then Johnson lifted two of Ma's speeches from the novel and had her say them both to Pa in the truck cab as they leave the government camp in search of work. One part of Ma's speech in the film was actually spoken to Tom in the novel in order to calm his murderous intent toward deputies and vigilantes at the end of the Hooverville episode: "We're the people that live. . . . Rich fellas come up and they die. . . . But,

Tom, we keep a-comin' " (383). The rest of Ma's speech in the film was spoken in the novel to Pa and Uncle John to urge them to just survive from day to day: "Woman can change better'n a man . . ." (577–8). Reportedly, Ford ended the film without this last speech from Ma but then Zanuck shot it and added it after the final cut, with Ford's approval.[20] Since the tone and meaning of Steinbeck's ending is itself hotly debated still, it is rather difficult to compare the endings of book and film; nevertheless, George Bluestone and Warren French came up with opposing views about the comparison. Bluestone, who sees the novel's structure as a parabola whose highest point is the government-camp episode, asserts that the film's

> new order changes the parabolic structure to a straight line that continually ascends. . . . the film's conclusion has the advantage of seeming structurally more acceptable. Its "new logic" affords a continuous movement which, like a projectile, carries everything before it. The movie solution satisfies expectations which are there in the novel to begin with and which the novel's ending does not satisfactorily fulfill. . . . If the film's conclusion withdraws from a leftist commitment, it is because the novel does so also. If the film vaporizes radical sociology, the novel withdraws from it, too, with Rose of Sharon's final act. The familial optimism of the one and the biological pessimism of the other are two sides of the same coin.[21]

Warren French, on the other hand, who has argued that the theme of the novel is "the education of the heart,"[22] asserts that in the film

> the emphasis is not on *change*, but *survival*. Actually in the film the only thing that the Joads have learned from their experiences is that they've just got to accept the beating they're taking and keep on plugging along. . . . The final point of the movie is exactly the opposite of the novel's. It is an insistence that survival depends not upon changing and dynamically accommodating one's self to new challenges, but rather upon passively accepting one's lot and keeping plodding along.[23]

In their attempts to coordinate the novel and the film these arguments oversimplify both works. Bluestone seems to miss the fact that Steinbeck's ending is multifold, complexly tying up the various levels of the novel — Rose of Sharon's act can be interpreted in many, many ways. On the other side, French seems to deny that

Tom, the major character of the film, has changed. There is a lesson here perhaps about the dangers of novel-into-film criticism: One often can gain more by immersing oneself totally in one work at a time. The progress of the film, apart from any knowledge of the novel, leads to Tom's speech, not to Ma's. The complex manipulative techniques of the film that I have described lead the viewer to accept Tom's and Casy's views of what the realities are and what the appropriate responses in the future must be.

In effective artful propaganda the ending is of great importance, because traditional closure can allow the audience to resolve and put aside the conflicts presented. The resolution of satisfying narrative is counterproductive to the intention to connect art and action in life. Many labor films have problematized endings as a result; for example, films with downbeat endings, like *On the Waterfront, Blue Collar,* and *Matewan* might be attacked for having descriptive rather than inspirationally prescriptive endings. In the other direction, the reassuring success of the unionizing in the inordinately upbeat *Norma Rae* ignores the important aftermath of the union's arrival: The company moved its plant away shortly afterwards, leaving these newly unionized workers unemployed. Simplistic storytelling conventions can work against developing political commitment in the viewer; only a complex ending will serve artful propaganda well. Certainly, this is one of the reasons that Steinbeck ended his epic abruptly with an enigmatic act that would keep the reader studying the world of the text. As he wrote to Covici, January 16, 1939, "I am not writing a satisfying story. I've done my damndest to rip a reader's nerves to rags, I don't want him satisfied" (L178).

Unfortunately for the film, Zanuck intended to deaden political outrage by adding Ma's final speech, an ending which many critics have pointed to as an incredibly inappropriate attempt to provide satisfying closure of the story and to undercut the radical messages of the film to that point. Yet, in spite of Zanuck's meddling, the film is quite open ended and radical, the ending more complex than he intended. The film actually has two endings since the sequence of Tom's leaving feels like the real ending. Tom's speech and mission look forward, bringing up new questions unanswered by Ma's platitudes. Ma is still wringing her hands and shaking her head while the family packs up to leave the government camp because no work is available in the vicinity. Before her supposedly reassuring speech, we see a long line of cars moving through an orchard that they dare not stop in or pick from, signaling the ongoing search for security in this Californian mirage of an Eden. Her platitudes about "the people" are no help against the lack of work, shelter, and food. Furthermore, Ma's speech can be read as continuous with her earlier asserting of necessary fictions to bolster the morale of the family. She is the uncomplaining maintainer of status quo in the home – in other words, the ultimate mother figure who not only attends to physical needs, but also works overtime to prevent the shattering of fragile psyches around her. The final speech of the film does not offer much closure; in fact, it is followed by one more shot of trucks moving along a highway backed by mountains and a sinking or rising sun. Since we can't know from the previous shots whether this is sunrise or sunset, the tension of hope and despair that has been presented throughout the film by sunlight and black night remains unresolved at the close of the film. In spite of Zanuck's attempt at closure, the ending leaves the tensions intact – of family survival pitted against labor organizing methods and of haves against have-nots. The film may not be able to muster the viewer's political energies (what artwork can move the unready?), but it does not allow the attentive viewer to shut off the connection between troubled protagonists and real-life struggling have-nots.

In his chapter about the migrants' search for pleasure, Steinbeck reminds the reader of two opposing audience expectations of Hollywood films. As a movie-going migrant tells another the plot of a screwball comedy, the other – more serious minded – interrupts him, saying, "I was to a show oncet that was me, an' more 'n me; an' my life, an' more'n my life, so ever'thing was bigger." The escapist moviegoer replies, "Well, I git enough sorrow. I like to git away from it." And the serious migrant replies, "Sure – if you can believe it" (446). The last sequence of Ford's film certainly caters to the escapist moviegoer, but the rest of the film's affective progress– its artful propaganda – is aimed at expressing the truth to the serious viewer, willing to make the leap into the Other's place and maintain the feel of that place even after the lights go up.

### NOTES

1. Pauline Kael, *I Lost It at the Movies* (Boston: Little, Brown and Co., 1965), p. 289.
2. Andrew Sarris, *The American Cinema, Directors and Directions 1929–1966* (New York: E. P. Dutton and Co., 1968), p. 45.
3. *Life*, (January 22, 1940): 29.
4. *The New York Times*, (January 25, 1940): 17.
5. *Steinbeck: A Life in Letters*, Elaine A. Steinbeck and Robert Wallsten, eds. (New York: Viking, 1975), p. 195. Subsequent references to this text will be indicated parenthetically, with L.
6. James Agee, *Agee on Film* (New York: Grosset and Dunlop, 1969), Vol. I, pp. 23, 31.
7. George Bluestone, *Novels into Film* (1957; rpt. Berkeley, CA: University of California Press, 1973), pp. 147–69.
8. Wolfgang Iser, *The Implied Reader* (1974; rpt. Baltimore, MD: Johns Hopkins Press, 1978), p. 59.
9. Lynne Tillman, "A Film with History," *The Independent* (January/February, 1987): 12–13.
10. Jackson J. Benson, *The True Adventures of John Steinbeck, Writer* (New York: Viking, 1984), pp. 408–11. Subsequent references to this text will appear parenthetically, with B.
11. John Steinbeck, *The Grapes of Wrath*, Peter Lisca, ed. (New York: Viking, 1972), p. 220. Subsequent references to this text will appear parenthetically.
12. William Stott, *Documentary Expression and Thirties America* (1973; new edition, Chicago: University of Chicago Press, 1986), pp. 211ff.
13. Ibid., p. 220.
14. Ibid., pp. 223–5.
15. Siegfried Kracauer, *Theory of Film: The Redemption of Physical Reality* (1960; rpt. London: Oxford University Press, 1970), pp. 240–1.
16. Tag Gallagher, *John Ford: The Man and His Films* (Berkeley, CA: University of California Press, 1986), p. 177.
17. Ibid., p. 178.
18. Vivian C. Sobchack, "*The Grapes of Wrath* (1940): Thematic Emphasis through Visual Style," *American Quarterly* 31(Winter, 1979): 612.
19. Ibid., pp. 609–11.

20. Gallagher, *John Ford,* p. 179.
21. Bluestone, *Novels into Film,* pp. 166-8, passim.
22. Warren French, *John Steinbeck* (New York: Twayne, 1961), pp. 97–108.
23. Warren French, *Filmguide to* The Grapes of Wrath (Bloomington, IN: Indiana University Press, 1973), pp. 25–6.

# Notes on Contributors

*Leslie Gossage* is an independent scholar working in film studies and feminism. She has taught English at the University of Virginia and has published articles on Lizzie Borden, Diane Kurys, and Margarethe von Trotta.

*William Howarth* is Professor of English at Princeton University. He is the author and editor of several books on American literature and cultural history, including *The Book of Concord* (1982), *Thoreau and the Mountains* (1982), and *The John McFee Reader* (1981).

*Nellie McKay,* Professor of Afro-American Studies and English at the University of Wisconsin, is the author of *Jean Toomer, Artist: A Study of His Literary Life and Work* (1984) and editor of *Critical Essays on Toni Morrison* (1988).

*Stephen Railton* teaches English at the University of Virginia as an Associate Professor. Author of *Fenimore Cooper: A Study of His Life and Imagination* (1978), he is currently finishing a study of the major prose works of the American Renaissance as performances.

*David Wyatt* is Professor of English at the University of Maryland, College Park. He has published *Prodigal Sons: A Study in Authorship in Authority* (1980) and *The Fall into Eden: Landscape and Imagination in California* (1986).

# Selected Bibliography

Benson, J. Jackson. *The True Adventures of John Steinbeck, Writer.* New York: Viking, 1984.

"Through a Political Glass, Darkly: The Example of John Steinbeck." *Studies in American Fiction* (1984): 45–59.

Bluestone, George. *Novels into Film.* Berkeley, CA: University of California Press, 1957; rpt. 1973.

Collins, Thomas A. "From *Bringing in the Sheaves* by 'Windsor Drake.'" *Journal of Modern Literature* (April 1976): 211–32.

Cowley, Malcolm. "American Tragedy." *New Republic* 98 (May 3, 1939): 382–3.

Davis, Robert Con, ed. The Grapes of Wrath: *A Collection of Critical Essays.* Englewood Cliffs, NJ: Prentice-Hall, 1982.

Davis, Robert Murray, ed. *Steinbeck: A Collection of Critical Essays.* Englewood Cliffs, NJ: Prentice-Hall, 1972.

DeMott, Robert, ed. *Working Days: The Journals of* The Grapes of Wrath. New York: Viking, 1989.

Everson, William. *Archetype West: The Pacific Coast as a Literary Region.* Berkeley, CA: Oyez, 1976.

French, Warren. *A Companion to* The Grapes of Wrath. New York: Viking, 1963.

*Filmguide to* The Grapes of Wrath. Bloomington, IN: University of Indiana Press, 1973.

*John Steinbeck.* New York: Twayne, 1961.

Kiernan, Thomas. *The Intricate Music: A Biography of John Steinbeck.* Boston: Little, Brown, 1979.

Levant, Howard. *The Novels of John Steinbeck: A Critical Study.* Columbia, MO: University of Missouri Press, 1974.

Lisca, Peter, ed. *The Grapes of Wrath.* Viking Critical Library edition. New York: Viking, 1972.

*The Wide World of John Steinbeck.* New Brunswick, NJ: Rutgers University Press, 1958.

Millichap, Joseph. *Steinbeck and Film.* New York: Ungar, 1983.

Motley, Warren. "From Patriarchy to Matriarchy: Ma Joad's Role in *The Grapes of Wrath.*" *American Literature* 54 (October, 1982): 397–412.

Owens, Louis. *John Steinbeck's Re-Vision of America.* Athens, GA: University of Georgia Press, 1985.

Pizer, Donald. *Twentieth-Century American Literary Naturalism.* Carbondale, IL: Southern Illinois Press, 1982.

Pratt, Linda Ray. "Imagining Existence: Form and History in Steinbeck and Agee." *Southern Review* 11 (Winter, 1975): 84–98.

St. Pierre, Brian. *John Steinbeck: The California Years.* San Francisco: Chronicle Books, 1983.

Shloss, Carol. *In Visible Light: Photography and the American Writer, 1840–1940.* New York: Oxford University Press, 1987.

Sobchack, Vivian C. "*The Grapes of Wrath* (1940): Thematic Emphasis through Visual Style." *American Quarterly* 31 (1979): 569–615.

Starr, Kevin. *Americans and the California Dream: 1850–1915.* New York: Oxford University Press, 1973.

  *Inventing the Dream: California through the Progressive Era.* New York: Oxford University Press, 1985.

Stein, Walter J. *California and the Dust Bowl Migration.* Westport, CT: Greenwood Press, 1973.

Steinbeck, Elaine A. and Robert Wallsten, eds. *Steinbeck: A Life in Letters.* New York: Viking, 1975.

Stott, William. *Documentary Expression and Thirties America.* Chicago: University of Chicago Press, 1973; rpt. 1986.

Wilson, Edmund. *The Boys in the Back Room: Notes on California Novelists.* San Francisco: The Colt Press, 1941.

Wyatt, David. *The Fall into Eder: Landscape and Imagination in California.* New York: Cambridge University Press, 1986.